T0357469

SPEAKING IN
TONGUES

ALSO BY

J. M. COETZEE

———

FICTION

The Pole

*The Museum Guard /
El Vigilante de sala*

The Death of Jesus

The Schooldays of Jesus

The Childhood of Jesus

Summertime

Youth

Boyhood

Scenes from Provincial Life

Diary of a Bad Year

Slow Man

Elizabeth Costello

Disgrace

The Lives of Animals

The Master of Petersburg

Age of Iron

Foe

Life & Times of Michael K

Waiting for the Barbarians

In the Heart of the Country

Dusklands

Siete cuentos morales

Three Stories

NONFICTION

*The Good Story: Exchanges
on Truth, Fiction
and Psychotherapy*
(with Arabella Kurtz)

Late Essays 2006–2017

*Here and Now: Letters 2008–
2011* (with Paul Auster)

*Inner Workings: Literary Essays
2000–2005*

*The Nobel Lecture in Literature,
2003*

*Stranger Shores: Literary Essays
1986–1999*

*Giving Offense: Essays on
Censorship*

*Doubling the Point: Essays and
Interviews*

*White Writing: On the
Culture of Letters in
South Africa*

ALSO BY
MARIANA DIMÓPULOS

——

FICTION

Imminence
All My Goodbyes
Quemar el cielo
Anís

NONFICTION

Carrusel Benjamin

TRANSLATIONS

El polaco
Capital y resentimiento
Modos del deseo
El tratado de Schelling sobre la esencia de la libertad humana
Filosofía y sociología
Benjamin sobre Kafka
Para una filosofía de la fotografía
Introducción a la dialéctica
Tres mujeres. Uniones
El París de Baudelaire
Parte de la solución
Correspondencia entre Walter Benjamin y Gretel Adorno

SPEAKING IN TONGUES

J. M. Coetzee

Mariana Dimópulos

Liveright Publishing Corporation

A Division of W. W. Norton & Company
Independent Publishers Since 1923

For information about permission to reproduce selections from
this book, write to Permissions, Liveright Publishing
Corporation, a division of W. W. Norton & Company, Inc.,
500 Fifth Avenue, New York, NY 10110

For information about special discounts for bulk purchases, please
contact W. W. Norton Special Sales at specialsales@wwnorton.com
or 800-233-4830

Manufacturing by Lake Book Manufacturing
Book design by Barbara M. Bachman
Production manager: Anna Oler

ISBN 978-1-324-09645-0

Liveright Publishing Corporation
500 Fifth Avenue, New York, NY 10110
www.wwnorton.com

W. W. Norton & Company Ltd.
15 Carlisle Street, London W1D 3BS

1 2 3 4 5 6 7 8 9 0

But that which is native to us needs to be learned just as well as that which is foreign.

—FRIEDRICH HÖLDERLIN

Contents

INTRODUCTION *xi*

CHAPTER 1

The Mother Tongue · *1*

CHAPTER 2

Gender · *31*

CHAPTER 3

Translating *The Pole* · *57*

CHAPTER 4

Words · *73*

ACKNOWLEDGEMENTS *101*

NOTES *103*

INDEX *105*

Introduction

THIS IS A BOOK ABOUT LANGUAGES: WHAT LAN-
guages can and what they cannot do. It was written
over a period of months by two hands in a dialogue form
and originated in a work of translation. Although it ad-
dresses some topics in linguistics, ventures into a few old
controversies, and aspires to some general statements, it is
not a work written by or for specialists. With no scientific
aspirations, it nevertheless enabled us to reach answers to
questions that appeared to be, during the months when it
was written, urgent, intriguing, worth being faced in depth.

The result was an amicable but intense discussion about
what we do with languages when we use them and when
we speak about them. In this, there is hardly any neutral
position to adopt. As soon as we become aware of this
ancient, profoundly human tool, we discover languages can
be loved, honoured, or treated with suspicion—and even
destroyed. Whether we qualify as humans because we are

able to speak is still a matter of debate. It is clear, however, that they constitute much of what we are.

During this exploration, there were a few issues that gained more prominence than others. Since the conversation emerged in the context of a translation, the problem of transferring literary and nonliterary content from one language to another was central. Soon it became clear that everyday activities such as writing, speaking, and communicating—usually thought of as natural and simple—are rather intricate. They proved to affect a great deal of how we think of ourselves and how we feel about others. They revealed themselves as pervading our emotions and determining the rules that govern our world. Individuals, nations, business, and science are partially made of language and of linguistic exchange. Books are published, sold, and read within a network of linguistic dominance. Thus, what languages are and what they are able to do is complex, fascinating, and sometimes unjust. Writing this work showed that common assumptions, such as what our mother tongue is, and forgotten premises, for example that natural languages determine our view of the world, may be worthy of being re-interrogated. Looked at with some persistence, even the use of the most simple of words such as *bread* or *rabbit* might turn out to be mysterious to attentive eyes.

In our first chapter, "The Mother Tongue," we discuss people who live a dual linguistic life, speaking their mother tongue among friends and family but using one of the "major" languages in public and professional life. Included among them are writers from "minor" language communities who conduct their writing careers in a major language. Is there not something uneasy about such a fate, we ask—having to work creatively in a language in which one can never be as fully at home as a native speaker is? Can one truly *love* the acquired language as we love the language we learned at our mother's knee?

Compelling children to speak the major language at school has proved to be one of the most effective means of suppressing regional dialects and imposing the ideal of the nation-state, with its single national language and its dominant national culture. Excelling in the major language is also one of the ways a young person gets ahead in the modern world—not just in the specialized world of letters and learning but in the wider world of business and commerce.

Yet this pressure towards monolingualism within the nation-state has its negative side: being able to inhabit a second language—as Friedrich Hölderlin argued—allows within us a certain distance from the world, an escape from a monolingualism in which the identity of *signans* and *signatum* seems unquestionable, "natural."

At a personal level, the histories of both our families include moments when the dialect or the minor language was given up and the dominant language adopted. In the case of one of us (JMC), retrospective doubts have begun to creep in about the wisdom of such a step—specifically about the adoption of the English language. These have led to experiments in the field of translation which are more fully discussed in Chapter 3.

What exactly is the status of a translated text? Does a

translation always occupy a secondary position compared with the "original"? Walter Benjamin argues that the summation of all translations of a work in some sense supersedes the original. In Chapter 2 we discuss approaches to certain inbuilt problems faced by the translator working between Spanish and English, such as the absence of social distance implied by the use of the English *you* in all contexts, or the extensive system of grammatical gender in Spanish, compared with English, in which the grammar of gender has almost vanished.

Why do certain languages, like Spanish, have gender differences built into them? To an extent the question is unanswerable, given that we have no historical materials to work with. The last serious attempt to address it was made by German philologists in the nineteenth century. To our forebears at the birth-time of human cultures, they argued, life was, down to its deepest level, sexed. The very fact that an entity might be classed as masculine in one language and as feminine in another was evidence, not that gender was assigned on an arbitrary basis, but on the contrary that each culture had its own unique world-view, realized in its language.

If each language offers its own, unique map of the universe and of human experience, how does the translator proceed when an item that is marked on the one map is not marked on the other? Does each language have its own semantic lacunae, objects or sensations that it fails to recognize? In simple cases the translator can paraphrase or import the foreign term as a neologism; but the problem becomes more profound when an entire grammatical sub-system, such as gender, is involved.

Gendered language has become a notable focus of attention today: feminists have called into question the dominance of a masculine norm, from which the feminine is treated as a deviation. Efforts towards reform of linguistic gender have proceeded in a number of languages. Whether language ought to be purged of all gender markers has become an issue in gender politics.

In the case of Argentinian Spanish, there has been progress towards neutralizing gendered language. Voices have been raised when plural forms such as *les* (in place of *los*) are used to avoid male bias: in some quarters there has been resistance against language being changed from above by a non-representative group of women. Though one of us (JMC) has reservations of a general nature about the engineering of language, we share a belief in the significance of the shift towards new, gender-neutral forms, where the political importance of the move seems to us to outweigh any violation of linguistic norms.

The case for reforming the gender system rests on the claim that the language we inhabit influences and even determines the way we see and think about the world. The claim that language—usually the language we are born into—dictates the way we see the world is radically opposed to the universalist position: that our perception of the world is independent of language.

Does the duty of fidelity that the translator owes to the text include fidelity to language that strikes her as morally objectionable (racist, misogynistic, . . .)? Is there room for a critical variety of translation which maintains a certain measured distance from the original? These and other questions belonging to the ethics of translation are taken up in Chapter 3. However, the core of the chapter concerns questions that came to the fore recently when a short novel entitled *The Pole*, composed in English by JMC and set largely in modern Spain, was turned by MD into a short novel in Spanish entitled *El polaco*.

The goal of this project was an unusual one: to make *El polaco* the "original" text, in the sense that all further translations would proceed from the Spanish text, not the English. This goal was largely thwarted by pressures from within the publishing industry, but the project allowed us to raise general questions about the secondary status of the translation relative to the primary or "original" text, and indeed about the secondary status of the translator relative to the primary status of the "originator," the author.

In a project in which the roles of author and translator were deliberately confounded, it fell to MD to create a Spanish text with echoes of English, especially in grammar—a Spanish that sounded slightly like English, and that readers would identify as foreign though still stylistically acceptable. Creating such a text was made more complicated by the fact that, although the text of *The Pole*, including all the dialogues therein, was in English, none of the characters in the novel, in the novelistic world in which they acted, spoke English as a native language. The dialogues of both *The Pole* and *El polaco* are therefore haunted by what speakers lack words to express, and even perhaps by what their mother tongues do not allow them to perceive.

This project had a political dimension too, arising from our growing concern about the global spread of the English language, including concern about the imbalance in the trade in translations worldwide: far more books are translated each year *out of* English than are translated *into* English. If this statistic reflects anything, it reflects a lack of curiosity within English-speaking countries about the wider world, in contrast to a (necessary? unavoidable?) attention on the part of the wider world to what the Anglo world is thinking.

In the final chapter we explore in greater depth the idea of faithful translation. To what should the translator try to be faithful: to the words on the page or to the intention that the translator infers behind those words? And when the translator goes further and stitches an interpretation of the text, or indeed in some cases a response to the text, into the translation, have the boundaries of translation proper been crossed and have we moved into the territory of adaptation or what the Romans called imitation?

The lead in the kind of interventionist translation here described was taken, decades ago, by feminist scholars of religion, who retranslated foundational religious texts, principally Christian texts, to soften their misogynistic bias and make them more hospitable to women. We cannot guess how long their versions will endure, but we do know that the neoclassical versions of Greek tragedy produced on the Parisian stage in the late seventeenth century tell us more about the France of Louis XIV than about Greece of mythic times.

At a more theoretical level, Chapter 4 takes up the question of untranslatability. Do languages and cultures whose histories have little in common interpret the data of everyday experience in radically incommensurable ways? Here the terminology of colour provides a convenient test cases: is the colour I call *azul* the same as the colour whose name a Spanish-Japanese dictionary gives as the Japanese equivalent of *azul*? Can we create an ideal, universal language, a language of pure meanings (so to speak), into which all existing human languages can be translated? And finally, how are we to interpret an experience well known to writers and translators, the experience of being sure that somewhere there is a word that corresponds to the idea in one's mind but being unable to find the word?

There is a major development in the general field of translation between languages that we do not discuss here, not because it is not of the utmost importance but because it is so new that no one is in a position yet to evaluate its limitations (if there turn out to be any!) when it comes to literary translation.

Artificial intelligence, conceived in the 1950s as an attempt to automate intellectual tasks performed by human beings, has now evolved into machine learning based on massive data sets. This crucial change has allowed machines to create their own rules, rather than acting upon given input using rules previously provided by their human programmers. For translation and other fuzzy tasks involving natural languages, fixed rules had proved inadequate in the past. Now, however, we can expect that automated translation based on machine learning will change the landscape of most text production. How far this development will affect literary writing is open to debate, but it would be naïve to think that translation practice and the book industry in general will remain untouched.

JMC

MD

SPEAKING IN
TONGUES

The Mother Tongue

J M C

In an ideal world each of us would learn to speak at our mother's knee. The language we learned from our mother would be our mother tongue. It would be the language in which the world is first revealed to us and would become the language of our heart. It would be the same language our mother learned at *her* mother's knee; and so on back through the generations.

When we later go to school, in this ideal world, we would be introduced to the grammar of our mother tongue, and read its literature, thereby deepening its presence inside us and its grip over us. Through its medium we would study science and history and philosophy. At a certain stage in our education we would begin to learn other languages too—learn to speak and read and write them, though never, by definition, as well as we speak and read and write our mother tongue. So we would learn that *khleb* is another word for bread, and *voda* another word for water. But if someone were to tell us that *bread* is another word for *khleb*, we would say, *No, you've got it wrong, it's the other way round.* Why? Because, if our mother tongue happens to be English, *bread* will be the *natural* word for bread; and the words of our mother tongue are, to us, the natural words for the way the world is.

But unfortunately this is not an ideal world, or at least not for all of us. In the less than ideal world that actually obtains, many of us, having learned our mother tongue at our mother's knee, and having received our first few years of schooling through the medium of our mother tongue, will thereafter continue our education through the medium of a larger and more important language, a national language like Hindi or an imperial language like English or Spanish. We will thus get used to inhabiting two linguistic spheres: the private sphere of the minor language, our mother tongue, which we will share with family and immediate community; and the public sphere of the major language.

To get our discussion moving, I would like us to reflect on the millions of people who live such a dual linguistic life, and specifically on those among them who make a living by writing. So I ask: What is it like to have Guaraní as your mother tongue but to make a living by reading and writing in Portuguese? What is it like to make a living by reading and writing in English when your mother tongue is Zulu?

I have two general observations to make about such representatives of the dual linguistic life. One is that they have an advantage over native speakers of imperial tongues, the anglophones and lusophones and so forth, in that from early in life they have absorbed the lesson that the world is not as it naturally seems, but rather is constituted for us by the language through which we apprehend it. The other is that they are uneasy beings who in their public life apprehend and represent the world through the medium of a language which, not being their mother tongue, is at some deep level foreign to them, a language in which they can never be at home as a native speaker is at home.

Such is the position of a considerable cohort of writers and intellectuals in the post-colonial world—in sub-Saharan Africa, in the Indian subcontinent, in Andean South America: people whose mastery of a major literary language like English or French or Spanish rivals that of native speakers, yet who do not know how to swear or make love in that language; who are fluent speakers of their mother tongue but stumble when asked to write in it. One can guess that for centuries, over the Roman Empire and the ex–Roman Empire, the position of male *clercs* was much the same as this: they read and wrote and even thought in some version of Latin, but spoke the vernacular in their intimate lives.

TO THE EXTENT THAT my analysis holds true, it seems to me to complicate the notion of mother tongue: for many members of the world intelligentsia, the mother tongue is no longer the language in which they do their thinking; yet at the same time in the language in which they think there inheres an uneasy foreign feel.

M D

To speak of mother tongues is to speak of origins. This question has been shaping our inquiries about languages for a long time, both in a personal and in a general sense. For centuries, speculations about language sought to discover a single historical root for all known languages. In the end, the idea was abandoned; but until that point the most striking candidates had been considered: first Hebrew, for obvious reasons in Western Christian thought, but then Gothic or German, and Chinese, even Swedish. The problem of origins was so persistent that an academy engaged in linguistic research had to officially declare that a single root of all human language was no longer to be pursued. A curious declaration, since science normally abandons matters of study not by fiat but by just dropping the thing silently. Probably, the question was regarded as unsolvable but still vexing. The image of a *Homo sapiens* talking to another in the twilight of a cavern had to remain blurred forever. Today, how languages originated is still a topic of investigation, but just for the most widely spoken, focusing on their development rather than on fixing an origin.

The perspective that we want to consider now is the private one. The language each of us learns in the earliest period of life is known, as you say, as our mother tongue or our "first language." This is the alternative origin, the origin of language that we can identify. Speaking of mothers and languages suggests an intimate scene: a toddler and an adult, a toy, something to eat or to drink. The child begins repeating sounds (*water!*), associating them with things and experiences—so the tale goes. Today we know that first-language learning begins at a very early stage, even during the first months of life. But it takes a long time for the child to utter the words needed to gradually become a dynamic part of its environment—which is more than eating and surviving. The objects named by the child are quotidian and simple. Names used by adults and learned by children leave an imprint on the world of their sentiments. Probably, we learn to *feel* a word in those first years, not merely to *use* it. We thus prefer the word *water* or the word *bread* just because we were, back then, open to the connection between feelings and words. We fall in love with words naturally in our first years. As adults, we can learn to love new words; but falling in love with them involves new efforts and new risks.

J M C

can guess what you mean by feeling a word or loving a word, but perhaps, for the sake of clarity, you should spell out your meaning.

M D

mean the kind of strong feeling that we have with some words that seem both natural and necessary to our ears and our hearts. This is an old debate whether the names we give to things are natural or conventional. But why? There are approximately six thousand languages in the world. It would be naïve to believe that the names each of us has learned during childhood are the exclusively natural correspondents to things around. So I can only imagine that in acquiring those names during our first years we simply "fell in love" with them. By love I mean a strong feeling of necessity, but a necessity that has nothing to do with rational thinking or logical inference. The metaphor also holds because love can be a cumulative process; later in life, we can learn to love new words for *bread* such as *khleb*.

J M C

Thank you.

M D

As with your first picture, mine is also idealized in many ways. Language is not, in real life, learned in an elementary scene with a caring adult and simple objects lying around, nor do we just feel strongly about words or fall in love with them. It is said that acquiring language begins even before we are born, and that it depends crucially on environment. Whether adults talk in front of the child and whether they take time to talk to their infants seem to be fundamental. The more the child evolves, the more complex the world around it becomes.

Language, first appearing as private, reveals itself as social. We still have our preferences, we pronounce our words in certain ways, we enjoy saying things, we understand each other thanks to language. Eventually, the number of people around—we call them family and friends—increases significantly. And the language that used to be coherent and unified and comfortable discloses its rules and exceptions. We begin to talk with unfamiliar people; we go to school.

What has happened? Mother tongue has become wedded to fatherland. This union has always existed in some way or other but has been institutionalized only in the past centuries. The marriage can be more or less forced. It seems particularly forced when our first language is not the official language, when at school we are compelled to learn a new and dominant tongue. How did this development occur? A dangerous—and false—idea took over the minds and hearts of statesmen, generals, educators, and others: that if a country wanted to be stable, unified, and prosperous, it should have a single official language. This is why the formidable process of teaching a significant part of humanity to read over the past two hundred years was both revolutionary and cruel. The child whose language did not coincide with the national language had to struggle in school, possibly suffering discrimination, because the song heard in those early years at home was not the same song intoned by others in the big world. This continues to happen every day to millions of people.

J M C

It is interesting that you pin down this process to the last two hundred years. I take it that you see the birth of the modern nation-state and the imposition of uniform national languages in schools as closely linked.

M D

Exactly. Although we know that there has always been linguistic domination, in the last centuries literacy reinforced the importance of the central languages, that is, those languages that ultimately prevail in multilingual social and political structures. States usually teach writing systems based on the dialect privileged by the central administration. Schooling is a great achievement; we don't want to disparage school attendance. It is only that, through early education, the mission of language, which is enabling people to communicate by giving them a common tool of expression, became something like a program of the state. Now we know that children that have late contact with the official language have a longer way to go to achieve the same level as the monolingual pupils. This is rather odd if we consider that the more languages we speak, the more capacities we develop, at least when trauma is not central in this process and when we are permitted to live with these two or more languages without constraints.

Reflecting on how complex this picture is, we understand why equating language with identity is a risky move. We have mentioned that first languages just sound natural to their speakers. Users do not only utilize words but also tend to think of those first words as the legitimate names for things around them. Faced with unknown languages, the sounds and words uttered by someone else seem just wrong, irritating, even menacing. From this perspective, of course, we can say that languages are constitutive of our identity. The ancient Greeks divided the world between "us" and "the barbarians," meaning by "us" those who spoke Greek and referring by "barbarians" to the ones that pronounced unintelligible words, those who said continually, to Greek ears, just "brbrbr." This portrait of a linguistic community being a monolingual "we" is far too simple. A German poet who also was a bit of a philosopher questioned the equation with significant acuity. His name was Friedrich Hölderlin and he grew up in the years when Germany was striving to become a unified country. Those were also the halcyon years of German philosophy, and he took part in the movement that reshaped the ways we think. He argued: What is mine, the most intimate feeling towards language, people, and landscape, is tinged and secretly shaped by things that don't belong to me. Identity is the result of a complex process rather than the absolutely defined shape of my own person. The same applies to any other kind of identity, for example cultural identity. Today we would say that cultural identities are the product of historical developments that can hardly be unified in a single source, that they are both domestic and originally foreign. Culture is many-faceted. It appears uniform and neat to our eyes, but this is only the surface. By reducing the sources of the self to a single "big" other, as German Romanticism was prone to do, the primal opposition between me and the Other, be it a person or a thing, vanishes. Hence, Hölderlin could say: I'm a mixture between myself and the other, even if I'm completely unaware of it; I'll never be really native to the things that are in my possession, starting with language.

This is a profound reflection on how we can feel trapped in what we are. We love and vindicate what we speak and, along with it, what is familiar and feels good. But the opposite experience is possible and not unusual. In that case we suspect that only in another language, a language we speak poorly, or a language we cannot speak at all, a foreign language, could we finally pronounce a truth that concerns us intimately. Writers know this feeling well, since writing, it has been said, is the experience of using our language as if it were a foreign one. It's just a metaphor, and a bit overused. But perhaps there is something to it.

JMC

You say that writing is the experience of using our language as if it were a foreign language. I have never heard that metaphor before, but I like it. It conforms to my own experience. I hope we will have an opportunity to return to it later, when we discuss literary language and translation.

However, let me concentrate here on what you have said about the (or our) mother tongue, where I have two observations to make.

First, how exactly does a child acquire language? This is a subject that has been much studied by linguists. There is one observation that I remember particularly well: that the baby's first attempts at vocalization, the stage that in English is called *babbling* (with reference to the tower of Babel), can in fact be interpreted as an exploration of the phonetic possibilities of our vocal apparatus. In other words, the newborn child enters the world capable of producing a range of sounds that has not yet been divided up between meaningless and meaningful (or potentially meaningful) segments—the child begins with the merely *phonetic* and progresses towards the *phonological*.

Similarly, the child begins life without a usable concept of the word—indeed, without a usable concept of meaning, of any linkage between the sound stream that issues from its lips and the world outside it—and then, by some complex process that undoubtedly (in human beings) has an innate neurological component, first constructs the notion of the word, and then, step by step, the system (which we call grammar) by which words are linked in utterances.

The point I am making here is that this process is not, or not yet, mother tongue acquisition, even though the child's real-life mother may be an intimate collaborator. It is instead an acquisition of *the idea of language itself.* Because one can't produce a sound in the abstract (the "idea" of a sound) or a word in the abstract (the "idea" of a word), the language that the child is in the process of acquiring is necessarily embodied in the language of the mother, but it is in fact language itself, not a particular language. That comes later.

M D

This is an intriguing and controversial issue. It seems well established that babies are not a tabula rasa when they start to learn a language. Humans are hardwired for language, linguists say. Scientific evidence shows that babies perceive vowels and consonants as categories, at least in the way that we, as speakers of alphabetically encoded languages, understand the difference. For there are different ways of encoding the sounds all speech is made of. We all "sing" something meaningful when we speak a language, but it depends on our writing tradition whether we describe these sounds as composed by "vowels" and "consonants" as we do, and it depends on each writing tradition how phonemic information is provided. Syllables, on the other hand, seem to be pretty much "universal," because speech sounds consist of forms of vibration (what we call vowels) and forms of obstruction (what we call consonants). However, this description can itself be biased. What we perceive as being educated in an alphabetic system may be our projection. By contrast, for example, Semitic writing systems tend to identify consonants and give less or no information about vowels, as in Hebrew or Arabic. In any case, it is said that babies are able to distinguish syllables that differ in only one of the phonemic information that we call "consonants." Take the pair of syllables "ba" and "da" in a given constant context. Babies' brains react differently to "ba" and "da," as do adult's brains—and this in every language in the world, no matter how these sound units are formally represented in a writing system.

In a first step, as you say, babies just train their vocal apparatus. Later, during the first year of life, they notice that some sounds are not used in their language, the language that has been around them since even before they were born. Within a few months, a baby's brain identifies which sounds are relevant to the language that matters. It also acquires the prosody of that language; it learns how to "sing" in the tongue that is also a linguistic destiny. As the neurolinguist Stanislas Dehaene puts it, babies behave like budding statisticians; through this mechanism, they identify certain words that occur frequently, obtaining this knowledge long before they are able to utter their first words. There is also a lot of learning of grammar rules in this period.

Babies are not only born with a certain linguistic ability. Neurolinguistics tells us that they also bring with them a sophisticated knowledge of objects, numbers, and face recognition. Among these very early and even pre-born skills, language shows a crucial relevance.

J M C

You referred a few minutes ago to the role of literacy—the capacity to read and write—in the growth of the nation-state. It is, of course, literacy in the national language that the nation-state promotes, not literacy in the abstract. The question I want to ask concerns not literacy, a term that pertains to individual speakers, but alphabetization, which pertains to languages themselves. Do you have any comments on societies that don't use the alphabet, societies in which the written language has no obvious relation to the spoken language or languages? I think in particular of China. Have speakers of the Chinese language(s) been more free to continue to speak the mother tongue, even as they learn to write and read the father tongue?

M D

The process of learning to write in Chinese is long and laborious because of the nature of logographic signs. Where there is no alphabet, the only option is to learn thousands of characters by heart. Here, there is an object assigned to each sign with no evident sound articulation. In logographic systems we recognize "things" or just meanings but get little or no information about pronunciation. The opposite happens with an alphabet, which works according to the principle of sound, by combining a very small set of signs (in the case of English, 26 letters) with a number of sound units. Letters are arranged in different ways to express phonemes, which are the basic sounds of a language. By following the pronunciation rules, we can "read" them. So if I know which sound is represented by a particular sign or a combination of signs, I can pronounce the word I read. Try the German term *Aufenthaltserlaubnis*; it looks like a nightmare, but as soon as you are familiarized with the appropriate phonetic rules, you are able to pronounce it correctly. Even in Western languages where phonetic rules are less clear-cut than

in German, for example in English or French, where sometimes many letters are needed to represent a single sound,
the system is the same. Think, for instance, of the many
letters needed to form the three phonemes of "thought."
What a word in an alphabetic system encodes is a sound
that conveys a meaning, turning the phonemic information
into phonological, meaningful particles. And if you have
enough phonemic information about the language in question, you will be able to read aloud a phrase of that language without understanding a word of it—just as opera
singers sometimes do. The contrary seems to happen with
Chinese characters: you would never be able to pronounce
it correctly by just reading, but you can learn the meanings of the characters, or at least of some of them—they are
said to amount to thirty thousand—without knowing the
language. However, in Chinese there are elementary units
of meaning that make easier the process of learning. That
logographic systems leave a greater margin for speakers to
be independent from writing constraints is possible, but this
does not mean that the power of written language as a sta-
bilising factor is less influential. What we do know is that
highly traditional, cumbersome writing systems make their
speakers live in a kind of diglossia, i.e., they write and read
in a language and speak in a simplified form of it. This is
the case with Chinese and Arabic. To be sure, the reason
why China introduced a simplification of its writing while
launching literacy campaigns in the 1950s and 1960s was to
make this process easier. The results have been contradic-
tory, experts say. Most central languages want to hold their

imperial grasp over their speakers in one or another way. Writing is an impressive device developed by humanity over thousands of years, a device that has worked incredibly well as an external memory. But it also has helped to centralize language and to marginalize both languages that have no writing systems and people who cannot use them.

J M C

Writing functions extremely well, as you say, to allow us to externalize memories, to record the past. But we should not forget that language is always moving, always shedding old ways of saying things and finding new ways. One of the effects of writing is to freeze language at a specific moment in its evolution, to slow down the pace at which it changes. In this respect systems of writing are in conflict with the inherent nature of language. This in turn has interesting implications for people who devote their lives to writing—not only writers (*escritores*) but scribes (*escribientes*) in general.

M D

You mentioned that you had never heard of the idea that literary writing amounts to writing in one's own language as if foreign. This takes us into the field of style. We usually think of an author's style as a highly personal achievement. Resembling a personal stamp, the way a writer puts words together is supposed to be what makes the writer's work unique. This is *her* language, we may say; this is undoubtedly *his* style!

The science of language says that, up to a certain point, each of us has some unique features that define our own way of speaking. Since we are able to communicate with others, however, it seems pretty safe to claim that, leaving aside small differences, we speak the same when we are within English, or Swahili, or Bengali—no matter how personal the way we arrange words into phrases might be. Anyone who has been in a situation where our interlocutor speaks a completely unknown language can confirm that being in the same language with others is rather beneficial, and most of the times a clear advantage.

Things are not that simple with authors. They write in one language, but in so particular a way that it may be argued they are operating in a language of their own. There is, for example, a controversy about Kafka and his German. It started with the work of one of his first biographers, who claimed that Kafka didn't speak German well enough, and that—paradoxically—the greatness of his literary art was the result of this limitation. Some years later, two French philosophers picked up the idea and invented a myth, the myth according to which Kafka had been the herald of a minor literature in which failures in the mastery of a language were a guarantee of authenticity.[2] This interpretation turned the works of the Czech author into a political machine. A rebellion of the bad speakers, we may say.

The metaphor of writing in our own language as a foreign one was first advanced by another French author, Marcel Proust. This idea turned the old concept of beauty upside down. Rather than attaining the most perfect expres-

sions and the most accurate vocabulary, a genuinely original author transfigures her or his own language so as to
make of it a new one. Literature used to be the product of
following ancient models, adapting old topics and rhetorical
forms for the taste and possibilities of modern ages. Later, it
became a personal product, and originality took the place of
perfection. From this moment on, a genius was a writer who
made a model out of his or her original beauty. We can say
that Proust's idea is a last variation on this theme. Originality becomes a matter of transforming literary language into
something remote and almost unknown.

The question is, why are we then able to understand and
admire such writings?

Beauty is a complicated matter; the pleasure obtained by
regarding, reading, or hearing artistic objects is even more
complicated. We have been taught that reading literature is
not just admiring a beautiful way of writing, and that literature offers an experience in which discomfort may be present and may sometimes become overwhelming. We know
about the problem of ugliness in art. In the Modern Age,
pictures started to portray unpleasant things and literature
to describe disgusting events. But there is another point
here, in my view. The idea of literary style changed fundamentally when readers and artists began to associate it
with originality rather than with the ancient rule of model
imitation. Perfection ceased to be a primary guiding principle. It has therefore been argued that great writers such as
Cervantes or Dostoyevsky wrote *poorly*, that their grammar
was flawed and their sentences inorganic, as if originality

would touch here on distortion. We can see these developments as the last output of the idea of literary style as a proof
of originality.

A final turn takes us to foreignness. Being extremely
conscious of the possibilities and limits of their language,
authors write in their own language as if it were a foreign
one. They treat familiar linguistic tools as if they were
unknown, with extreme care and attention. The simplest
sentence can be then considered difficult. This is why Kafka
wrote somewhere in his diaries that the most difficult thing
was to make a character leave a room by simply writing,
"He left."

J M C

I want to return to the question of the mother tongue, and
to the story you tell about the child who learns one language
at home—the child's mother tongue—and is then made to
speak another language at school—the father tongue. We
are obviously moving here into the political dimension of
language.

On this theme, let me say something about my personal
linguistic background, and the linguistic background of the
family I come from. It is a history that might at first seem
complicated, but, I would argue, is in some ways represen-
tative of the world of the twentieth century.

On my mother's side I am descended from a Pole who
left Europe in the 1880s. Born in Prussian-ruled Silesia, he
decided early in life that the future was German. Accord-

ingly, he Germanized himself by changing his name, attending a German school, and marrying a German girl. Their children, born in the United States, spoke German at home and English in public. From the United States they moved to South Africa, where they continued their bilingual German-English practices, even though they were now living in a Dutch-speaking environment. What I have told you is thus a story of how, for the sake of social advancement, a mother tongue—first Polish, then German—was abandoned in favour of a father language, first German, then English.

On my father's side I am descended from people who migrated from the Netherlands to the southern tip of Africa in the seventeenth century. During the Napoleonic Wars this little Dutch colony was taken over by the British, and its inhabitants became subjects of the British Crown. My ancestors accommodated themselves to their new masters, conducting their public life in English while continuing to speak Dutch at home—Dutch which, in its heavily creolized form, would become known as Afrikaans. Again we have a story of a mother tongue—Dutch—being abandoned in favour of a more powerful father tongue, English.

M D

The picture you give of South African linguistic conditions, as illustrated by your personal story, has some points in common with the linguistic impact of European immigration into Spanish-speaking Argentina, which took place

between the 1870s and the 1930s, with a second peak immediately after World War II. The other crucial event of linguistic merging in South America had, of course, already
taken place; it was the outcome of Spanish and Portuguese
colonial immigration and the resulting linguistic pressure
on the languages of the indigenous peoples after the Con-
quista, that is, during the seventeenth and eighteenth centuries. Later, in the nineteenth century, when nation-states
took over the "mission" of standardizing central languages
and subjugating indigenous populations through language,
the process of partial fusion and general domination became
official policy. Only in the last thirty years have a series of
new regulations in Peru, Bolivia, Paraguay, and Argentina
started to reflect the multilingual reality of these countries.
With its plan for a new constitution, Chile sought to pur-
sue a similar path. Take Argentina as an illustration: there
is evidence of fourteen languages spoken in its territory,
although there are few bilingual schools where teaching is
practiced both in an indigenous language and in Spanish.
Migrations coming from China, Korea, and Russia in the
second half of the twentieth century challenged the monolingual system in new ways.

Coming back to European immigration, the history of
my family may provide a good example. My mother was
born in Spain and immigrated with her parents, brothers, and sisters to Buenos Aires in 1950. On this side of my
genealogical tree, there have always been people who spoke
with a slight Peninsular accent, and who never mastered the
autochthonal use of the second person in the Argentinian

vernacular—but no more than that. My father was born in Argentina but his parents were both Greek. He came in contact with Spanish on the streets of his neighbourhood even before his schooling and learned to speak this language with no accent. With his sister and mother, however, he always spoke Greek, a language he never taught to his own children. When my grandmother grew very old, she forgot Spanish, a language she had learned when she was about thirty-five but never mastered; I remember going to visit her with my father and just watching them interacting in their tongue, in dialogues I couldn't understand a word of.

Is the role of Spanish in Argentina as my story pictures it to be compared with the role of English in South Africa?

J M C

believe so. I believe the parallels are enlightening.

In my case, to both the maternal and the paternal sides of my family, English—the master tongue—seemed to be the way of the future, and an English-language education the best way of ensuring that a child would prosper. Both of my parents had their schooling in English, and learned to read and write English better than they read or wrote Afrikaans.

The language of schooling remained an intensely political issue. By the time I arrived on the scene in the 1940s, the reactionary Afrikaner nationalist movement was on the point of taking over political power. The current that had borne so many Afrikaans speakers into anglophony began to be reversed; and a cohort of children like myself was left stranded, at home neither among the Afrikaner-nationalist majority nor among the suddenly powerless Anglo minority.

The phenomenon of which I was an instance—the child who masters the English language but is not a member of the Anglo culture—was not uncommon across British colonies in Africa and Asia. As British control weakened and withdrew after 1945, significant minorities were left behind: middle-class "natives" who, attracted by the material advancement promised by British-dominated commerce and government, had done their best to anglicize themselves. Even in their isolated position in the newly independent nations, such minorities continued to feel they belonged to a worldwide Anglo culture, whose centre was perhaps now the United States rather than Britain.

M D

These developments are specific to South Africa, but they offer a clear example of how the conflict between languages can quickly become political.

How did this constellation influence your life as a writer?

J M C

As a child at school I found that I was "good at" English. I seemed to have an intuitive feel for the language. At the age of seventeen I enrolled to study mathematics at the University of Cape Town, but also took courses in Latin and in the subject called "English Language and Literature."

Founded on the values of British Liberalism, the University of Cape Town was the institutional embodiment of a belief, so deep that it barely needed to be articulated, in Progress: humankind was on a progressive historical trajectory, and by a decree of divine Providence the British race had been entrusted with leading that upward drive. In my courses in English I competed successfully with Anglo South African classmates: I knew their language, it seemed, as well as they did. After graduating I went to live and work in London, heart of the old Empire. I adapted my colonial way of speaking and my colonial manners; with my white skin I could soon pass undetected in the crowd.

After years in England I moved on to the United States to continue my education in the humanities. I graduated with a doctorate and returned to South Africa, where I was hired to teach English language and literature at the same institution whose portals I had entered as a student fifteen years before. There was a certain historical irony in this return: with not a drop of English blood in my veins, and with an abiding scepticism about the ideology of Progress, I was being entrusted with conveying the values enshrined in the English language and its literature to the sons and daughters of Anglo South Africa.

I became a writer too, an "English" writer in the sense that I wrote in the English language, though—to use your metaphor—I treated the language as if it were foreign to me. I wrote novels, which were published in New York and London, the twin centres of English-language publishing. Since I was neither American nor British, my books were listed in their catalogues under the catch-all title "World Literature."

I was also widely translated, at a time in history when many more books were translated out of English than into English. Why was this so? The answer I received from the industry—that English speakers were on the whole not curious about the "outside" world—was only partly true. A fuller answer would have been that English speakers could afford to be indifferent to the outside world, whereas the outside world could not afford to ignore the Anglo world, and in particular the United States. Thus it was only natural that foreigners should want to translate books from the Anglosphere into their own languages; whereas to be translated from a foreign language into English was a mark of distinction. As the United States had become master of the world, so the language of the United States had become the language of the world. One could travel the globe and "get by" with English. Foreigners learned to speak English, that was the rule; it was not really necessary for Anglos to learn foreign languages.

I visited Iceland and in Reykjavik met two adolescent boys, sons of my host, who told me, in excellent English, that they disliked their native Icelandic: the language was too difficult and anyway had no future. The future belonged to English. They sounded to me as I must have sounded a generation earlier. Perhaps they too would end up as professors of English.

At more or less the same moment I began to question my position in the system, as an assimilated foreigner whose very mastery of the master language seemed to confirm that it was only natural that English should rule the world. I had always felt foreign in Anglo culture, felt like an imposter. Now the language I spoke and wrote—spoke and wrote so well that it could have been mistaken for my mother tongue—began to feel foreign too. Foreign to me, and foreign to Africa too, where it had never taken root, had never tried to take root, had remained the language of the masters from across the seas. The language of my books began to take on a more abstract quality. I had lost interest in sounding like a native—that is, a native English speaker.

What was going on? I told myself I was feeling my way towards a rootless language, a language divorced from any sociocultural home. If I had known Esperanto, if I had been confident that Esperanto had the expressive resources I needed, I might at that moment have turned to writing in Esperanto.

I had always checked translations of my books when they were translated into languages that I had some knowledge of. Now I began to work more closely with my translators, with a new interest in hearing how I sounded outside the English language. I also began to ask myself why the versions of my stories that my translators produced had to faithfully follow the English, why they had to carry a label saying that they were not the original story. Did a translation necessarily have to have a secondary status, the status of an imitation (an imperfect imitation) of a unique original?

M D

This is a point often contended among translators. But originals exert a fascination all of their own beyond this particular field; this a phenomenon that does not only concern translation. Take a canvas by an oil painting master, for example; it is immensely more valuable than a copy, even if the normal human eye would never tell the difference. Just as in reproductions of a work of art, in translation there is the undeniable temporal order in the relation with its original. Reproductions and translations come always afterwards. It is impossible to reverse this order, even when the first text has disappeared and only translation has survived—something that is not uncommon in old manuscript traditions, or in paintings, or in sculptures.

Walter Benjamin, the German critic and philosopher, wrote a brief theory of translation that elaborates upon this well-established idea. The title of his essay is "The Task of the Translator." Here, Benjamin considers translation in the long run, as a vehicle for the afterlife of literary works of art. Given the temporal nature of languages—they are perishable just like any other thing alive—a piece of writing that has never been translated into a new language will eventually vanish with the tongue in which it had been originally written. So translation is a guarantee for the persistence of a set of texts, called classics, translated over centuries from their original versions to new and more vivid languages.

Having explained this process in the historical dimension, Benjamin extends the picture to the end of time. Then, he turns his description into a speculation about linguistic expression—just until the point in which history is over. He argues that being translated, the classics would perfect the languages into which they are reproduced so that eventually all ever-spoken tongues would end up becoming a single ideal language. In his view, this will be the language of truth, a language with no traces of "terrestrial" limits.[3]

Giving works of art a new wording involves, for Benjamin, the destruction of originals with the aim of perfecting natural languages through the art of translation.

J M C

Over the years my German translator, Reinhild Boehnke, has produced text after text in German that, in my eyes, are in no respect inferior to the English texts I have written. If she and I were to switch roles, if her text were to appear in German under her authorial name and then later my text were to appear in English as a translation out of her German, would our ruse be detected? I doubt it. As her translator, I would be praised for the accomplishments that translators are usually praised for: fidelity to the original, mastery of idiom, et cetera.

At last we arrive at the point in this long biographical excursus where our paths first cross, yours and mine. I first met you when, for an anthology I was preparing, you translated some stories by Robert Musil from German into Spanish. At the same time, with the backing of our sympathetic Argentine publisher, Maria Soledad Costantini, I was embarking on a series of collaborations, initially with Elena Marengo, then with you, turning English texts that I had written into Spanish texts that were intended to carry no marks of a secondary status: where my English proved recalcitrant to Spanish reformulation, it was the English that had to give way and be rewritten.

It was no accident that these collaborative books were published first in Argentina, then later on in Australia, two countries of the southern hemisphere. (I call it the southern hemisphere, not the Global South, a term I avoid.) They appeared first in Spanish, just as the afterworld in which my three Jesus novels are situated is a Spanish-speaking afterworld—Spanish-speaking not because I think Spanish is in some sense "better" than English, but simply because Spanish is viable as an alternative to English (also because I thought it would give a jolt to Anglo readers to find that the language of the afterlife would not be English). These collaborative texts appeared first in Spanish, and they appeared first in the southern hemisphere. Thus they did not first have to pass the scrutiny of the gatekeepers of the North (editors, reviewers) before they could be read in the South.

In this way we come to *The Pole*, which first saw the light of day in Buenos Aires in 2022, in the version that you prepared, and then in Australia in 2023, before making its appearance in the North.

M D

It is this exceptional attitude towards translation and publishing that makes of that book a unique project. We have already mentioned that translation cannot reverse the order of things: first comes the original, then the translation. From the beginning, however, *The Pole*'s project suggested that it is possible to invert the order of things, at least in some way. And, for me, this transformed the whole task of translating it to its roots.

Gender

J M C

Let me start with one of the most frequently remarked upon differences between English and Spanish (also English and French, English and German, . . .), namely that in Spanish the social and/or personal distance between speaker and addressee is marked, whereas in English it is not. In Spanish you say (speaking to a man), either *[Usted] está bienvenido* or *[Tú] estás bienvenido*, the choice depending on the speaker's sense of his distance from the addressee (also on his sense of the addressee's sense of their distance). In English you say (speaking without distinction to a man or a woman), *You are welcome.*

In translating *You are welcome* from English to Spanish— let us say in a work of fiction—the translator [*la traductora*] has to decide how to mark the distance between the two actors: is it a formal or intimate? In most cases the context will provide an answer. But consider the case of two characters whose relationship has started, like most relationships, on a formal footing, but has then by steps become more intimate. The moment of transition from formal to intimate is not marked in the English, where the actors address each other as *you* from the beginning. Therefore the translator has to intuit the arrival of this moment. In fact, she has to intuit something going on under the surface in the lives of the two characters that the author has not articulated and may not be fully aware of. In this respect she has to know more about the characters than their author (consciously) does, and to make a semi-authorial contribution to the text.

This recurrent problem—how to identify the moment of transition from formal to intimate when translating from a language in which distance is unmarked to a language in which it is marked—is well known in the profession of translating. Less well recognized is the inverse phenomenon, which occurs when you are translating from a marked language to an unmarked language—from Spanish to English, for example. One might think the matter is simple: both *[Usted] está* and *[Tú] estás* become *You are*, and that is the end of it. But reflect on real life, life outside the text. How does the native speaker of Spanish feel, who may be used to welcoming a stranger with the formula *[Usted] está bienvenido*, when a monoglot English stranger arrives and he has to consider whether or not to utter the English formula *You are welcome*? Does he not perhaps feel a twinge of uneasiness, a feeling that, addressed to a stranger, the formula is overly intimate, too close to *[Tú] estás bienvenido*? Might he not therefore prefer to circumvent the troublesome word *you* by using an alternative formula, for instance: *It is a pleasure to welcome so distinguished a visitor?*

Consider now a reader reading a translation into English of a Spanish novel in which a host greets his English visitor with the words *Es un placer dar la bienvenida a un visitante tan distinguido,* words which seem to translate "It is a pleasure to me to welcome so distinguished a visitor." *What a wordy man this host is!* the reader will think to himself; or else. *What a pompous language Spanish is! We English would simply have said, "You are welcome."* The motive behind the host's wordy formula can be guessed at by any intelligent reader of the Spanish original, namely to avoid violating a social norm, but is obscure to the reader of the English translation.

What steps can the translator can take to avert such a misunderstanding? There are two I can think of, and both are radical. One is to add an explanatory gloss: " 'It is a pleasure to welcome so distinguished a visitor,' said the host, thus avoiding the over-familiar *you*." The other is to treat the Spanish locution *Es un placer dar la bienvenida a un visitante tan distinguido* as a social formula, and to translate it with an English social formula: "You are welcome." In the latter case the translator takes on an active role, *nativizing* the host's words.

The problem created by *you* as opposed to *Usted/tú* (or *vous/tu* or *Sie/Du*) is only a special case of what we can call the specification problem. The writer [*escritor*] who writes the sentence "Roger and his brother caught a bus" believes

that his words are clear and unambiguous. But to his Vietnamese translator [*traductora*] they are not. There is a word
for "elder brother" in Vietnamese, and a word for "younger
brother," but no word for "brother" per se. The translator has
either to work out from the context whether the brother in
question is older or younger, or else has to contact the author
and ask, "Was Roger's brother older or younger?" To which
the author may very well reply, "I don't know and it does
not matter." But how can he not know when, at the moment
when he wrote the sentence, he must have had a mental image
of two boys getting onto a bus, one of them bigger and therefore older than the other? "No," says the writer, "my mental
image was not of a bigger/older boy and a smaller/younger
boy, it was just of two boys. You fail to understand what one
does when one writes fiction. One does not give a complete
account of the world in which the fiction unfolds, an account
that includes the relative ages of the brothers, the colour of
the bus they catch, the weather on that day, et cetera. On
the contrary, one records only what is necessary within the
economy of the story. Therefore," continues the writer, "you,
the translator, must decide for yourself which brother is the
older, it is a matter of indifference to me." The translator dis-
agrees but holds her tongue. She fails to see how one can have
a mental image of the two brothers catching a bus and yet not
know which was younger, which was older.

If it so happens that the story is adapted for the screen,
the specification problem recurs in an even stronger form,
for the director responsible for casting the actors needs to
know the ages of the brothers, just as, ultimately, the film

needs to know the colour of the bus and everything else that the author could have had in mind but did not when he composed his troublesome sentence.

The author specifies what he deems necessary within the economy of the story. The decisions he makes about what to specify and what to ignore are aesthetic decisions. But in the medium into which his story is translated (a book in the Vietnamese language, a film) these aesthetic decisions are necessarily overridden by down-to-earth considerations. There are no plain brothers in Vietnamese; there are no colourless buses in cinema.

What Roger and his brother provide is *not* an instance of untranslatability—it is important to make this point. There is a way of saying, in Vietnamese, that two boys, children of the same parents, caught a bus; there is a way of filming two boys catching a bus without making the colour of the bus visible. These roundabout ways of saying "Roger and his brother caught the bus" preserve the level of specification of the original story, adding nothing that its author deemed unnecessary, and therefore in a certain sense translate it accurately; however, they do so at the expense of violating the stylistic simplicity of the original.

M D
⸺

The specification problem is the real problem of linguistic equivalence, and linguistic equivalence is the crucial problem of the whole science of language, a linguist once said. I think he was right. Here you give us a striking example.

Languages differ in surprising and sometimes annoying ways. The absence of marks of distance in interpersonal treatment in English are dreadfully missed by translators into Spanish or German, as you point out. What is interesting here is that it is not necessarily so when one speaks the language, even as a non-native speaker. In English the difference is still there, but the speaker rarely think of needing two pronouns for reflecting it. In my view, this is a telling distinction. This is a reminder of something usual but nonetheless disturbing. It is a reminder of how comfortable we may feel in a language as long as we do not compare it with another one.

Translation, however, is exactly that: comparing languages and making the best of it. According to some theories that have been particularly successful, we do not translate languages but only sentences or texts. This position is as calming as it is inaccurate.

Especially in literary translation, it is the whole system of differences, nuances, and resonances of words that needs to be translated, finally defining the quality of the resulting text. Of course, this is an idealized picture (again!), but this is how it should be: trying to figure out what an author does to his or her own language so that not only the content of an expression is rendered in the new linguistic context but also that resonance.

Comparisons—and translations—are not always easily avoided. Of course, we can live our whole life imagining we need no translations, although our present world tells us the opposite. From a historical perspective, however, translations have been rather marginal over centuries. Only when several languages came together in a relatively close space and exchanges accelerated did speakers become aware of their own linguistic tools. And then they compared. This happened, for instance, some four hundred years ago in Europe. According to this example, which is the most significant for Western languages, speakers tend to note first the deficiencies in vocabulary of their own language. So did English speakers before the huge movement of lexical acquisition that ended after Shakespeare. What the inhabitants of old Europe thought of themselves and of other speakers is still interesting for us; it provides a model of the "anxiety of languages."

One can argue that experiencing the lack of a word is rare and irrelevant to everyday life, but in translation these questions are unavoidable. When we are faced with the absence of a word in the target language (that is, the language into which we are translating something), we can create a neologism, or borrow a word, or offer a rephrasing. Every translator knows this kind of comparison with the linguistic tools deployed in the original text. So we search for equivalences, compensation, and other remedies. But things get extremely difficult when the opposite is the case, especially in grammar. Now we have an abundance of information in the target language rather than a deficiency. Your translator into Vietnamese was faced with the demand of her own language, that asked her for a difference which grammar does not require from English speakers. In English, you are free to imagine the two brothers without answering the question of who is the older one. You have presented this freedom as a right to stylistic simplicity that should not be violated by translation. Your statement is a reminder of how important the balance between information and silence can be in literature, and how important it is to pay tribute to it in translation.

Where do all these constraints forcing the provision of more information than originally given come from? Grammar is like an old bureaucratic machine that has forms to fill in; it makes language understandable and consistent by giving tools to but also by placing restrictions on its users. In this sense, it is correct to say that it affects our world-view in some way. What is important here is that you can perfectly express in English that a brother was older (or the other younger), only that it takes more words to say it, and you are not forced to do so. Grammar machines are sensitive to some information while showing utter unconcern about other; grammar can make us lazier sometimes. Or, as you put it, it can make us free to opt for simplicity.

J M C

There is an arena in which the question of specification has taken on unusual urgency in our time. This is the arena of gender. In its simplest form, the charge is that many of the languages into which human beings are born have a system of gender specification which is built into the language despite being redundant for basic communicative purposes. Thus when we read the English sentence *The doctor took the king's temperature* we do not know and do not need to know whether the doctor was a man or a woman. When that sentence is translated into Spanish its gender-blindness ought ideally to be maintained—the translator should not have to choose between *El médico* and *La médica*. If we erect gender-blindness into an overriding principle, then the Spanish language ought to be purged to bring it into line with English: no gender marking by suffixation (*-o/-a*), no gender marking by article (*el/la*), no gender marking by pronoun (*el/ella*).

In this example, the English language happens to figure as the gender-blind ideal. But even within English, gender marking can rear its head. *The doctor took the king's temperature, after which (he? she?) inspected his tongue*: as soon as the anaphoric third-person pronouns (*he/him/his, she/her/her*) come into play, gender has to be specified, even in English. At this point Turkish, a language without grammatical gender, may need to replace English as the ideal.

Whether languages ought to be brought up to date by being purged of gender markers is no longer just a question to be deliberated in language academies. It has become a political issue, an issue in gender politics. Whether languages ought to be purged of markers of social distance is parallel question, though much less urgent.

Here I wish to tread a delicate path. While skirting the battle over gender in language, I wish to raise three questions that are immediately relevant but are usually passed over. (1) Why do (some) languages have a gender system? (2) What, if anything, would be lost by the erasure of gender from language? (3) By what means would the erasure of gender be effected? In exploring these questions, I will take my examples mainly from two languages: Spanish, which has a gender system that has survived more or less intact over time, though it has lost the third gender (neuter) of Latin; and English, which in its present form (Modern English) has lost most of the grammatical gender system of Old English.

(1) Why do some languages have gender; or, to put the question in a more technical form, why do some languages divide nouns into classes and treat these classes differently at a grammatical level (for example, certain nouns can be replaced only with the pronoun *he* or *él*, other nouns only with the pronoun *she* or *ella*)?

The short answer is, We do not know and will never know. We will never know because, by the time writing was invented and records were kept, the languages in question were already flourishing with their fully developed gender systems. No history of language-use exists that goes back far enough in time to give us the evidence we need.

Ought we then to abandon the question of why (some) languages have gender? Not necessarily, as long as we are prepared to delimit the question in such a way that it can be usefully explored, and as long as we are clear about terminology. What exactly is gender, and what exactly does the word *gender* mean in a linguistic context?

Here is a rudimentary definition of the term *gender* as used by grammarians: gender is system that allocates all the nouns of a language to one of two, or sometimes three, classes; the first two classes bear the traditional names *masculine* and *feminine*.

The definition is careful not to state on what basis, *if any*, a noun is allocated to a class. However, the traditional titles *masculine* and *feminine* (plus *neuter* if there are three classes) create problems. Consider the case of a visitor from Mars who is presented with an alphabetical list of all the Spanish nouns that are preceded by *el,* side by side with an alphabetical list of all the Spanish nouns preceded by *la*. It is by no means obvious that the alien would identify the common feature of nouns in the first list as biological masculinity (possession of XY chromosomes), and the common feature of nouns in the second list as biological femininity (possession of XX chromosomes), assuming for the moment that these are the only chromosomal alternatives. A more cautious definition of gender would therefore avoid biology and speak only of noun classes (Class 1 and Class 2), eschewing the provocative terms *masculine* and *feminine*.

But *gender* is not solely and simply a grammatical term: it is also a term in social thought. Depending on what school of thought one belongs to, one's gender is one's sex, or the social role to which one is allocated on the basis of one's sexual characteristics, or the sexual-social role that one chooses to inhabit, or the set of sexual-social behavioural patterns that one adheres to.

M D

In linguistic comparison gender is one of the most prominent issues today. Your three questions give us a practical device for a measured account of the problem. This problem is a thorny one for us. Before we go further in the exposition, it might be useful to draw a distinction between gender marks in nouns referring to inanimate objects and gender marks in words referring to animate ones. From the perspective of languages in which noun classification is not depending on gender marks such as English, it is puzzling that a table should be *feminine*, or hair should be *masculine* as it happens to be in Spanish. But assimilating the two kinds of nouns into gender in general would be misleading. As you point out, grammarians have arrived at the conclusion that grammatical gender is a category for classifying nouns as any other. The problem is that a classification of nouns in which gender is only a name (and therefore could be replaced by Class 1 and Class 2) can be mistaken for a classification of the objects referred by those nouns. So that we may think that a table has some feminine attributes because it is called *la mesa* and not *el mesa*. An additional problem is that, for animated objects that are sexed, the gendered classification does apply to both nouns and the objects referred by them. In German, you say *die Schildkröte* for the turtle, although there are male turtles as well.

But grammarians insist: the fact that these two (or sometimes three) categories got the names of *masculine* and *feminine* (and *neuter*) can be just seen as an unhappy decision by our linguistic ancestors. What these marks provide is grammatical information about how phrases are built, and nothing more. Through these marks, elements can be distributed in a sentence more freely than in languages with

fewer markers such as English. Just think of the extreme
freedom in arranging words in a Latin phrase.

This does not mean that gender is completely absent in
such languages as English, even beyond pronouns such as
him or *her*. Think of the difference between ram and ewe,
for example. Spanish can also distinguish between feminine and masculine in some few animals that proved important for human feeding and survival (*carnero* and *oveja*, *vaca*
and *toro*).

This offers further support to the idea that gender classification originally worked the other way around. In Spanish, for example, first there was noun endings in *-a* or *-o*
and, later, the classification was assumed to be gendered.

J M C

The overlapping and intersecting uses of *gender* as a grammatical term and as a social-sexual term are confusing
enough. Further confusion ensues when we translate the
term out of English. The Spanish word *género* has a range of
meanings: grammatical gender but also, more broadly, type
or genre or (in biological science) genus. Addressing the use
of *género* to signify what US feminists mean by *gender*, the
Mexican anthropologist Marta Lamas writes:

> The feminist academy of North America advocated
> an interpretation [of gender] as relating to inequal-
> ity between women and men, and *gender* in this sense

was rapidly "universalized" by the mechanisms of globalization available to the North American *doxa*.

To Lamas, the new signification to be attached to *gen-der/género* is not so much a gift from the US academy to the world as an instance of "the academic hegemony of North America" imposing itself on the world intellectual community.[1]

Similarly, defending the understanding of relations between sex and gender developed in Scandinavian feminism, Karin Widerberg questions whether the analysis of gender coming from the USA holds true for societies elsewhere. She goes so far as to envisage a gap of untranslatability between sex/gender as understood in Scandinavia on the one hand and in the USA on the other. When they are translated into English, she writes, Scandinavian concepts "get made into something else, into the understandings of gender that are implicit in the English language."[2]

Lamas and Widerberg alert us to the possibility that the feminist critique of language emanating from US universities may have less of a universal reach than it claims to have: that it is, in essence, a critique of the English language insofar as English is the instrument by which U.S. culture and society understands itself.

The case for reforming the gender system in language rests on the claim that the language we inhabit determines or at least influences the way we see and think about the world. This claim is commonly known as the Sapir-Whorf hypothesis or the linguistic relativity hypothesis. In the view of Edward Sapir (1884–1939), gender is a quality we *impose* on an object of perception rather than a quality we *detect* in it: we impose gender on objects of perception "because of the tyrannical hold that linguistic form has upon our orientation in the world."[3] There is no perception, no world-view outside of or prior to language: language comes first, organizing our perceptions according to its own logic, including the logic of gender.

The claim that language—usually the language we are born into, our so-called mother tongue—dictates the way we see the world is radically opposed to the universalist position: that our perceptions of the world are independent of language.

M D
—

Just one word on the impact of gender discourse—or any discourse—that may come from a centre of knowledge production such as the USA in present times. According to a well-accepted idea concerning the history of science and discourse in general, scientific truths are both the effect of a structure of power and have as an effect some structure of power. This is a rather pessimistic but accurate view to some extent. An example may illustrate how the supposedly neutral and perfectly ahistorical truth is just an ideal. We can imagine a scenario of someone staying alone in the middle of a rain forest, let's say, a genius in some science. This person utters a general truth of the universe. Now we may ask the following question: Would a genius who pronounces an indisputable truth in the middle of a rain forest a single time have any chance of having pronounced an indisputable truth? Since truths are historical statements made in historical contexts, the answer might be negative. Contexts in which truths are uttered have an impact on how truth is known, up to the point of both imposing it on others or, in the opposite case, making it disappear. Contexts are so relevant that they can even shape uttered truths, for they may condition both their authority and their reception. In our case, a discourse about gender pronounced in English and read and commented on by a number of peoples around the world are the conditions in which this kind of discourse has emerged and circulated, with all its far-reaching consequences.

Of course, the prominence of the context for any discourse is greater when the knowledge in question particularly depends on linguistic means, since any knowledge must be uttered in a natural language in a specific social environment. This is the case when gender discourse meets the critique of language. Because of an extraordinary capacity of languages to refer to themselves, this critique turns out to be helpful when we reflect on the language employed to express our thoughts. And English being the language in which the discourse about gender has been lately articulated, distinctions are naturally drawn from it. Experts reflect on their use of their own language and draw conclusions from it. However, things can become too biased by language. The more self-reference in a critique of language we have, the less independence of contextual constraints we obtain. For example, if I write "This sentence expresses no gender" and try to universalize it as an example of lack of specification through gendered marks, I will fail. Just try to translate it into Spanish and you will find out that gender is still there, at least grammatical gender.

J M C

In languages with two gender classes, nouns referring to beings of male sex usually fall into one class and nouns referring to beings of female sex into the other class. Speakers of two-gender languages are expected to attend to sex distinctions in their daily life, and, when dealing with human beings (more rarely with other living beings), to perceive the referents of nouns as either female or male. Psycholinguistic experiments tend to support, or at least not to disconfirm, the claim that such speakers conceptualize not only human beings but objects in the real world, and abstract concepts too, as in some sense "possessing" gender, masculine or feminine.[4]

The compulsory bipolar gendering of human beings—compulsory because built into the gendered language—extends beyond gendered nouns and the gendered pronouns (anaphoric pronouns) that can stand in their place, to include systems of concordance according to which gendered nouns require similarly gendered adjectives. Binarism affects the lexicon too, often in a non-symmetrical way: the masculine verbal form is the norm, the feminine the deviance. Thus *los niños* are children and also boy-children, while *las niñas* are children too, but only insofar as they are girl-children; a *poet* is a person who writes verse while a *poetess* is a woman who writes verse.

A question that immediately arises is whether this formal imbalance in favour of the masculine-gender norm has real-life powers. Do human beings who submit to the prevailing rules (rules of grammar, but also rules for getting along in society) grow used to accepting that the feminine is not the norm; do women who follow the rules grow used to inhabiting a secondary role?

If we accept that language does indeed have the "tyrannical hold" over the mind that Sapir ascribes to it, and that the masculine-gender norm imposed by language is undesirable, then the logical next step would be to divest the language of this particular bias by reforming its gender system. What need do we have for gender, after all, when it is clearly non-functional (there are languages without gender) and may even be dysfunctional (in discriminating against half the population of the world)?

But how is this operation on the body of language to be performed? Is gender a relatively superficial feature of language, a feature that we can easily and successfully excise; or does it lie so deep that we cannot cut it out without changing the language fundamentally?

The question of why gender is inscribed into language has intermittently exercised thinkers since the time or Protagoras (circa 490–420 BCE). The last occasion when it was treated as a serious topic of inquiry was in the heyday of German Romanticism, when philologists taking their inspiration from Johann Gottfried Herder's 1772 essay on the origin of language argued that the system of gender enshrined in a language allows us unique insights into how our remote forebears saw the world. At the birth-time of human cultures, argued such scholars as Jacob Grimm (1785–1863), our forebears animated the world, brought it to life, through language; and life, to them, was down to its deepest level, sexed. The fact that an entity might be classed as masculine in one language and as feminine in another was not, to such scholars, evidence that gender assignment was arbitrary but on the contrary evidence that each culture had its own unique world-view, given form in its language.[5]

There has been renewed interest in our own times in the question of whether gender assignment is arbitrary, that is to say, lacking method or logic. Psycholinguistic studies of perceptions of gender suggest that native speakers of a gendered language tend *not* to regard grammatical gender as arbitrary: they implicitly claim there is a semantic quality shared by most masculine nouns on the one hand, and a different semantic quality shared by most feminine nouns on the other, though they may not be able to articulate what that quality might be other than masculinity or femininity. In the Indo-European languages there appears to be a corpus of non-animate entities (objects, states, concepts) that uniformly fall into the masculine gender class, and another corpus that uniformly fall into the feminine class. For instance, *sleep* (*el sueño*) is uniformly masculine, *religion* (*la religión*) is uniformly feminine. Since not all of the nouns in these corpora go back to prehistoric times, there is a suggestion that gender assignment is not arbitrary—that some classificatory operation may be at work whose logic is unclear to us.[6]

I am now in a position to return to the question (2) as enunciated above: What, if anything, would be lost by the erasure of gender from language? The answer would seem to be: something that speakers of gendered languages know, or feel they know, about the world, even if they do not know it consciously; where *knowing* is to be understood not as a passive absorption or ingestion but as an act of the mind, possibly a projective act.

WHICH LEADS US TO question (3): How could the erasure of gender from language be effected? A provisional answer would seem to be: with ease in some languages, with difficulty in others.

The lead in the drive to purge language of gender has been taken in anglophone countries, principally the United States. It is no accident that this is so: Modern English possesses only fragments of a gender system, and the basis of that system is semantic or "natural" rather than grammatical. There is no linguistic construction in English that presents the conflict between grammatical and natural gender that we see in French, in a sentence like *Madame de Sévigné est un grand auteur français.*

Why English lost grammatical gender is a question for historians of the language to decide. The prevailing notion in the popular mind is that the story of English is a story of steady evolution from unnecessary complexity to rational simplicity. But perhaps there was no steady evolution at all, from Old English through Middle English to Modern English: perhaps in the Middle Ages there occurred a rupture on such a scale that Modern English is tied by only the thinnest of threads to Old English.[7]

Whatever the case, it would, in the abstract, be no difficult task to rid English of the remnants of its gender system. How one would accomplish a purge of any residual sense of gender in the minds of English speakers is a separate question.

M D

As you have mentioned, experimental psychology has been examining the influence of gendered grammatical distinctions in speakers' choices and conceptions. The results are not always as consistent as we might expect. Whether a speaker of German would choose adjectives associated with male features for inanimate nouns only because of the grammatical gender of that noun (assigning "masculine" attributes to a table just because it is *der Tisch*) seems to be dependent on the method of analysis. From the perspective of someone who grew up in a gendered language, the plausibility of assigning just "feminine" attributes to a table—just because we say *la mesa* in Spanish—is rather low. The important question here is whether the argument of contamination speaks for or against a general movement of neutralization of linguistic gender.

Coming to the point of male bias, there is enough evidence for supporting this idea. With this term we mean the fact that gender neutral expressions generally convey masculine contents, so that a word describing an undefined person would automatically describe a man. The bias can be reinforced by grammatical gender, as you say. So that if I want to stress that a poet has been recognized as the most significant in the past 30 years and that poet happens to be a woman, if I choose the expression *poetess* I could be understood as meaning that she was the most significant *exclusively among woman-poets*. On the contrary, if the poet is a man-poet, the same sentence using the supposed "neutral" term *poet* would induce the interpretation that this man-poet is the best of poets *in general*, unless we accept gendered judging in art as a rule.

I suggest examining this problem in the light of universals and the question of their validity. Are there really universal truths and assertions? There are well-accepted and powerful claims said to be universal. The universalist position is commonly associated with male dominance. As long as something is not marked as being "special", it works as a general statement and probably as masculine. Since women historically depended on male predominance, they got used to accepting this mechanism. This pervades culture and society, going far beyond language. In my view, much of the effectiveness of (false) universal positions is that they are built upon the contrast between marked and non-marked items. This means that the marked items are *not-universal* as long as they differ from the norm that claims universality. So that, following the example of the poetess, she would never be the best of her generation in general but only among women.

Today, how we should react to this state of affairs is the subject of debate. Schematically, there are two ways of fighting false universalization. One is creating tools, new linguistic tools in our case, that are not marked. The other is proclaiming differences and politically transforming differences into identity, and identity into a proof of the falsity of universals. The method is supposed to show how weak is the ground universals are built on. Both options are well represented among feminist thinkers and activists.

Finally, I would like to come to your last question. There is some scientific evidence that new grammatical tools for expressing gender neutrality actively defuse potential male bias. So while traditional expressions such as "the applicant" would suggest to a majority of readers that the candidate to a job position is male, the use of "he/she" or gender-neutral new forms as *ze* would neutralize the gender-associations in the reader's mind. Just an example coming from the South: In Argentinian Spanish the options for neutralizing gendered language considerably increased in the last few years. The movement found many supporters and was prompted by feminism. But several voices were raised when plural forms such as *les* were created to avoid the male bias of the plural form *los*. Some people were afraid of having the language changed from above—and only by a non-representative group of young women. I think this is not the right way of having it. I prefer to interpret all uses of new gender-neutral creation rather as a political statement in which linguistic norms are a second range problem. Here, the point is drawing attention to the fact that language is not a neutral tool, especially in social questions. And that, to a certain extent, we can modify it.

This leads us back to question (2). As a native speaker of a language in which grammatical gender is dominant, I'm acquainted with the following two experiences. I can tell how unimportant the grammatical gender of a spoon is, and I also realize that in some cases, as you say, the gender of inanimate objects seems far more relevant. This is the case of some nouns that can arguably be conceived of as universal, such as *sun* or *moon*. For Spanish speakers, the sun must be masculine and the moon feminine.

However, as it usually happens, comparison with other languages sobers our ambitions of universal representations. Just think of German and its feminine sun and its masculine moon. In an influential article, the linguist Roman Jakobson once argued that grammatical gender of celestial bodies conditions mythical representations for each language. Some years later, the anthropologist Lévi-Strauss took issue with the claim and wrote an article with the suggestive title "The sex of heavenly bodies."[8] He stated that all types of gender and familial relationships had been attributed to the moon and the sun in aboriginal languages across the Americas. In some they are a couple, in others they are brothers, in others the one is a by-product of the other. Grammatical gender does not always coincide with mythical contents, he stressed. However, it seems improbable that language would not serve at least to enhance mythical representations.

I assume that, from the perspective of a language in which gender is rather marginal, the arbitrariness of linguistic gender can be both annoying and fascinating.

J M C

I grew up speaking two languages, Afrikaans and English, both of them more or less bereft of gender. At school I was introduced to gender through Latin. Like my schoolmates, I regarded the phenomenon of grammatical gender in a way that now strikes me as lamentably blind: as a tiresome means of complicating a language for complication's sake. Not once did I ask myself—nor was I encouraged to ask— why the Latin language was as it was. When I later acquired a smattering of German and French and, later still, of Spanish, I continued to regard gender as a feature of language without a function which I nevertheless had to take note of at the risk of becoming a laughing-stock whenever I opened my mouth.

It is only recently that I have begun to wonder whether I was not missing something: a window to a universe not of objects but of forces, forces which to our ancestors (here I adopt the story told by Herder and Grimm) were ultimately versions of the great procreative drives, the masculine and the feminine, embodied and embedded in language since time immemorial.

Languages have histories, but those histories are in large part beyond recall, so far back in time do they go; or, if one prefers an archaeological metaphor, so deeply buried do they lie. From those relics that have reached us from the buried past—of which the gendering of names is one—we can guess—but do no more than guess—how the world must have seemed in those days.

Which is why I wonder, in turn, whether full translation is possible between a gendered language, whose speakers may still, in an obscure way, feel the presence of archaic forces in the world around them, and a genderless language, from which those forces are excluded.

Translating *The Pole*

M D

When translators come together, there are two topics that might guarantee a spirited conversation. They can speak about the works of others, usually in a slightly critical vein, and they can talk about the painful task they are sometimes, if not most of the times, subjected to. Translation, all agree, is hard work. In these exchanges, they do not differ much from writers *tout court*, but in the case of translators the feeling of community prevails over the exhausting game of vanities. No matter how flattering this analogy might be for translators, there is a radical difference between writing a book out of nothing, progressing line after line over a blank page as writers do, and composing acceptable, even aesthetically pleasing strings of words when that page is already full of the words of another person. This simple fact draws an undeniable line distinguishing one activity from the other. Since I alternate between the two positions, as many writers and translators have done and do still today, for me this is simply an empirical fact. Writing is one thing, translating is another. And there is some comfort in this fact. Even if we know that translations are sometimes saddled with important responsibilities—think of medical directions of use— the idea that we are not alone, that someone is behind us, is reassuring in translation. One can always argue: It was the author who did it, not me; there is something to be said, and I'm just helping to make it known.

From the beginning, translating *The Pole* was something different from that. The idea that the Spanish version would be the only version available for some time—something I was informed about from the beginning—would always be present, accompanying in subtle ways all my decisions of translation. Why? The precept had taken a radical turn in me. I thought of the book in Spanish as the original for all translations in other languages to come, even into English, as if the original manuscript had vanished. Of course, this was a thought experiment, and eventually things went the usual way. But the idea wouldn't leave my mind, effacing the promise of that comfort of not being alone once the book was published.

Although frequently considered a marginal activity, translation is disrupted by weighty ethical questions. A translator makes decisions in the solitude of a room, even if comforted by the thought that, at the end, her version will be just a version of an original that looks over her like a benevolent, protective mother. As long as the book is not yet published bearing the name of the author on the cover, her decisions are taken in seclusion. At that point, and because of the many decisions to be taken, the question of liberty arises. To what extent may I move away from the original? Is it still translating if I'm too liberal and creative? In the case of *The Pole*, the idea of making a "new original" restricted these liberties to a minimum instead of multiplying them. So I was trying instead to write a text in Spanish that had English remnants, especially in grammar, as if my text was a tracing map drawn on tracing paper like the ones we did in school before digital life began. A Spanish that sounds slightly like English, that later readers would recognize as foreign but still acceptable, even graceful if I was skilled enough.

But things were not so simple. The fictional characters depicted in this novel written entirely in English speak sometimes in Spanish, and sometimes in English as a second language. The illusion of fiction makes it possible; nobody would complain about the absence of Latin in any filmed version of the victories and tragedies of Julius Caesar. Since none of the characters in *The Pole* has English as a mother tongue, their use of this language is flawed, sometimes evidently so, at other times in elusive ways. Several voices coexist in the sober narrative of *The Pole*. This raised the urgent question about the number of layers of implicit translation a novel can accept. Translation is the game of making explicit many things while covering some others with a mantle of discreet elegance. This is the reason why dialogues played such an important role in this case. I had to make them intentionally awkward, but in the right dosage and at the right moment. As soon as this challenge had been met, a late paroxysm of multiple linguistic intricacies was waiting for the translator and the future reader at the end of the book. The story ends with a poem written in Polish, rendered into Spanish (but we read it in English!) by an Italian translator who lives in Barcelona. A carrousel of mirroring linguistic allusions.

There was, however, some relief on other fronts; the typical difficulties of literary translation were reduced to a minimum. Let me explain. Each natural language has a special music, a particular taste for images, and an array of preferred structures that fixes words as in a gold chain. If someone lets the cat out of the bag in an English sentence, it can mean that someone allows a feline to escape from its prison or that someone reveals a secret unintentionally. In *The Pole* there were very few passages in which ambiguities, complex sentences, or huge metaphorical images prevailed; the prose of the novel has been imagined as transparent, almost detached from all traits that could identify it as English, as if the old *genie de la langue* had been intentionally kept in his little bottle.

Fortunately, soon after I had completed the translation the spell of being alone was broken. The novel in its Spanish version was discussed line by line with you, a few passages adapted, a few additions approved. With this, the old order of things was restored—at least for me.

J M C

As you observe, the English in which *The Pole* was composed is unusually bodiless and unlocated: it is not at all obvious where in the world it comes from (given that English is used as a medium for writing over much of the world today), and it lacks the solidity (semantic but sonic too) that characterizes most high-quality literary English.

There are two reasons why the book inhabits this null linguistic state. The first is that I deliberately starved it of what I think of as native nutriments while I was composing it. The second is that, by the time I began to compose it, I had reached a point in my life where I was seriously concerned about the English language as a global political force, and wished to emphasize my personal rupture with it.

I will discuss these two factors, and what lay behind them, more extensively later on. For the moment, let me just observe that your fantasy that you were composing the book, in Spanish, for the first time—that you were in a sense its author—was not unfounded. It was my intention that no translation—no "good" translation—of the book should be inferior to the English, and thus that the notion of an "original" version of *The Pole/El polaco* could be brought into question. As legal copyright holder of the story, and therefore in a sense its "owner," I intended that the English text, once it had metamorphosed into the Spanish text, would retire for a while, withdraw into the shadows, while the Spanish text would give birth to a multiplicity of translations.

However, this plan was defeated by a superior force that operates in the world publishing industry. Publishers in Poland, in France, in Japan and other countries simply declined to translate from the Spanish text. The Spanish text, they said, did not constitute the original, and they preferred to translate from the original. In fact, it was an article of faith with them that one should translate only from the original. Thus I reached an impasse. For eight months the only version of the book that existed in public was the Spanish one, which was treated like any other Spanish book in the sense that it was reviewed in Spanish-language periodicals and bought by Spanish-speaking readers.

I have no doubt that if the book had been composed in Albanian and translated into Spanish, publishers would have been prepared to abandon the original-language principle and commission translations from the Spanish. Why then the impasse? The answer: because the "original" was not in Albanian, a "minor" language, but in English, a "major" language and indeed perhaps today's master language. In the contest that I provoked with the original-language principle, and implicitly with the master language itself, I lost and the principle prevailed.

There are two other points, in your account of how you wrote the Spanish text, that I would like to take up.

The first is that you briefly reflect on the question of what duties the translator owes to the text. Does she have to be faithful to the text under all circumstances, or is she free to diverge from it now and again and follow her own desires? For example, is she free to improve the text where it is clumsy or graceless or obscure?

Here let me observe that you are not the first translator to give voice to this question. The question has come up most forcefully in relation to older texts, where the author is dead and the entire structure of language and meaning has begun to shift with the passage of time. Should the translator of a nineteenth-century text try to reproduce the language that a contemporary nineteenth-century translator would have used? More significantly, should she reproduce the more unconscious features of the text with a deliberate unconsciousness of her own, or should she bring them into relief? I am thinking here of matters of race. If the nineteenth-century text unreflectingly or unconsciously reproduces attitudes towards race typical of its times, attitudes that might today seem racist, should the translator faithfully and obediently replace the original with its verbal equivalent in her own language, or does she have a moral, historical duty either to highlight what is going on—to bring it to consciousness, so to speak—or even to censor it?

A second comment. In a film set in ancient Rome, you observe, we do not expect Julius Caesar to speak in Latin. But—a thought experiment—would it not be interesting if Shakespeare's *Julius Caesar* could be performed in a hypothetical Latin two thousand years old, subtitled for our convenience in our own language? We might learn a lot from the experience, principally about points of untranslatability between Caesar's time and ours, points at which the Romans are irretrievably alien to us.

M D

There are some essential points you raise here. I would like to address the one concerning untranslatability later, and for the present focus on the issue of the "language order." I will also comment on the ethics of translation below.

There are two different ways of thinking about language orders, at least two ways especially relevant to our discussion. In translation, you have a natural language order that is simply temporal. You have a first language, which is the language of the original, and you have a second language, which is the language of the translation. But there is another dimension in language orders that is as important as the temporal one. It concerns the range of cultural, political, and symbolic importance. This immediately brings up the question of which factors determine priority. An obvious answer works partially in this case: the more people speak a language, the more important that language is. English being the most important language nowadays, it is also correct to say that it is the most spoken in the world. However, the point here is that a large proportion of English speakers are not native speakers. If we were to take into account only the ones that have English as mother tongue, Mandarin, Hindi, and even Spanish would be equally qualified. The rise of English—just as the rise of any other language in the world order—is a historical phenomenon; it took a crucial impulse only in the twentieth century, displacing French from a strong dominating position. Alongside French, Latin still played an important role well into the nineteenth century. Even Dutch was once widely used in diplomacy and trade. Before that, Spanish dominated. Because of our globalized world, however, the scope and predominance of English's reach today has no real precedents.

What does it mean that there is an order of languages? Well, not only that it is more practical for everyday life to learn English rather than Croatian as a second language; that you will be able to communicate with far more people speaking the former than the latter. What seems crucial here is the fact that languages are always associated with ideas and representations, feelings, and judgments. We hardly have a neutral attitude towards any language. We associate particular languages with positive and negative ideas, no matter whether we speak it or not. There is an illustration to this that is both funny and accurate. It is a famous anecdote about the linguistic abilities of Charles V. As the emperor of the Holy Roman Empire during the European Renaissance Charles was said to speak Spanish with God, Italian with the courtiers, French with his mistress, and German with his horse. We can see from the language order held by the minds during the Renaissance that linguistic prevalence is variable. English wasn't even mentioned as an illustration of anything in those days, at least not in the main version of the story.

Although the study of vernaculars began with the rise of Latin in Antiquity, there is, for us, a turning point in the late Middle Ages. Five hundred years ago European languages became visible to their users and makers. All kinds of new speculations and ideas were entertained about them. Richness or poverty of vernaculars was discussed, pondered, and mocked. Languages inspired opposing sentiments: for their users, European languages both suffered from a shortage of words and rejoiced in the copiousness of expressions.

Sometimes other speakers possessed the better language and sometimes it was the other way round. Spanish, French, English, Italian, Dutch, and Portuguese: their strength, their beauty, their faults were heatedly debated. Grammars and dictionaries were written in honour of the chosen ones. It was always at the expense of some other dialect that national languages were established. Are plenty of designations for one thing a sign of development or rather of primitiveness of a language? In the centuries to come, the same argument would be raised in favour or in condemnation of a language. At the beginning of the Renaissance, when the whole process of the battle of vernaculars was set in motion, a Spanish savant called Nebrija articulated a truth about language prevalence that is still valid today, namely, that languages can rapidly become a vehicle of oppression and conquest. Empires were built through force and linguistic imposition; languages persecuted, prohibited, and erased.[1]

J M C

There is a variant of your anecdote about the Holy Roman Emperor in which he adds that to his accountant he speaks English. If English has spread around most of the world today, it is as a medium for commerce rather than because the world yearns to read Shakespeare in the original.

It would be inaccurate to say that imperial languages like Spanish and English are spread by force among subject populations. Much of the time, subject peoples adopt them when they recognize that they will never flourish in the new commercial economies without the master's language. They learn the master's language as a second language; then, within a generation or two, it takes over as their primary language, usually in a creolized form.

M D

You mention the duties and liberties of translators, and you ask about the balance between the two. This concerns, of course, not only the people who make their living translating texts, conversations, legal documents, or medical information, but also the ones who rely on such information and exchanges. Because of the global shape of our world today, a great number of us vitally depend on the results of translation. Consider, for example, the high proportion of information about products, tools, culture, and news first expressed in some language other than our own. From the English perspective, the proportion of translated materials is less than, say, the amount of information needed in translation by speakers of Albanian. The reason is that English has so deeply pervaded the production of both material and intellectual goods that we write our operating instructions and our scientific papers directly in this language—no matter in which linguistic contexts the goods have originated. Still, the knowledge of history, sociology, and many other sciences and experiences of men and women depends upon information given in hundreds of different languages all over the world, and those words uttered by men and women need to be understood—and translated.

In literature, things are more complex. Whereas in the translation of a medical information leaflet being accurate can save lives, in literature fidelity to the content appears to be less important. Was the character's t-shirt blue or black? Is this information relevant for our understanding of the novel in which a marginal character wears a t-shirt with this or that colour? Well, it may be relevant, but this strongly hinges on the story being told. In literature, we may say, there are no absolute values of information. What is crucial to the narrative can only be stated at the end of the story. In literary theory, this is sometimes called Chekhov's Gun. This narrative principle was first put forward by the Russian author as a clue to what is relevant in a story. If a gun is hanging on a wall at the beginning of a story, someone will have to take it down at the end. The principle has had many variations over time; the version I first heard of was more peaceful, talking about a nail on the wall and a picture someone hangs on it at the end. This is why we can say that whether the colour of that t-shirt is relevant to the story in translation is only visible at the end, inviting us to take a more holistic view.

Personally, I see the principle of fidelity always hovering over the heads of translators. A translator can make a lot of mistakes trying to be faithful to her original, but the risks are higher if she tries to free herself from the constraints of her guide-text—even with the best of intentions. When we talk about the ethics of translation, the first point is figuring out what the balance should be between fidelity and freedom because, in my view, the scale cannot constantly tip in favour of being literal. In literary translation, honouring a text also means being creative to render some kind of beauty, regularity, even the author's intention (is there something like this?) in my own language. This is utterly impossible if the translator restricts herself to translating literally.

But there is another, ethical point to be made, a point that you mentioned. Since the aim of translation is transposing information and contents from one language to another, this is exactly what a translator should do. But when this information is ethically dubious or objectionable, then the one principle of faithfulness collides with the higher principle of what is worthy to be made known. You would not accept a novel to translate that expresses racist content. But what about a passage in an old text? I think that here the text has a right to be known as it is. It would be a mistake to make old texts just as we want them now. It is sometimes difficult, I admit.

An example: The first translator of Anne Frank's Diaries into German changed a passage where the young author, writing about relations between Jews and Germans in the terrible context of her seclusion, says something very negative. In the 1950s, the translator thought that was exactly the wrong message to pass on, and played down the content of Frank's strongly worded assertion. But from our perspective, the translator was possibly wrong. The first principle of the ethics in translation should have prevailed over the second.

J M C

am not sure that the German translator of Anne Frank was wrong. One can argue that, in Germany of the 1950s, when the nation was trying to crawl back from years of barbarism to membership in the circle of civilized nations, though flames of resentment against the victors were still crackling under the surface in some quarters, messages of reconciliation were needed, not messages of hostility. If this was the view that Anne's translator took, then he or she was acting more as a cultural mediator than as a translator *stricto sensu*.

Perhaps—and this is only a tentative suggestion—a similar principle ought to operate today in the publishing and translating of those classic texts in which there is language that now strikes us as offensive in one way or another—racist or anti-Semitic or homophobic or whatever. Perhaps we should yield to pressure from offended parties to blank out such language, and rely on the pendulum of history to swing the other way, to a day when the author's original language can be restored.

In literary translation, as you say, getting the literal meaning across, word by word, is not an absolute value. Nevertheless, in prose fiction, where the formal structure of the text is not complicated, we can normally expect a strict standard of fidelity. Poetry is different, particularly poetry where patterns of sound and stress carry a large quotient of meaning. Here the translator is continually having to juggle the claims of the literal meanings of words against the values of those words in a landscape of sound and tone.

In the case of *El polaco*, which we talked about before, the demands on the translator are unusual in one respect: much of the dialogue in the story (and here I want to distinguish clearly between story and text) is carried out in English, which is the first language of none of the protagonists. The translator therefore has the difficult task of conveying in Spanish those moments when speakers struggle to find words or get the words wrong or even cannot say what they want to say because they cannot find the right words.

M D
—

want to come back briefly to the Romans, Julius Caesar, and Shakespeare. Your suggestion about translating Shakespeare's English back into Latin is provocative. For me, it is a reminder that we can interpret human experience and ethical and political problems in no matter which language they are expressed. Curiously, the idea has already been put into practice. A short stroll on the Internet tells us that Shakespeare's play has a Latin version. What can we learn from taking a look at this version? If we read the play in search of historical information and Roman context, I think it may be worth a try—in case we have learned some Latin. But the experience suggests that the version also sounds a little whimsical, perhaps because of the loss of significance and dignity suffered by Latin in the last decades. In the end, the Latin version seems to be just a joke.

And a last remark on old languages and originality. Writing in English, Shakespeare does introduce some Latin in his piece in a critical moment. For when Julius Caesar recognizes his former protégé among the conspirators, he utters "Et tu, Brute?," which means something like "You too, Brutus?" Then he covers his face and dies. So these are his last words, and last words are a topic in itself. We know, for example, the last words said by Goethe. *Mehr Licht!* he whispered, asking the ones at his deathbed to let more light enter into his bedroom. According to versions circulating since Antiquity, what Julius Caesar said to Brutus was not in Latin, that is, in their usual language, but in Greek, the language of culture in Rome. He is said to have exclaimed something like "You too, child" or "You too, my son." Why did Shakespeare put Latin words in the place of Greek ones? Important here is that he used an ancient language instead of English. He thought, probably, that Greek had in times of Caesar a similar status to Latin in his own time. The dramatic effect seems to be the same. In this sense, he was more faithful to truth by telling a lie, that is, creating something new.

J M C

We know little about the real-life William Shakespeare, but one of his contemporaries observed that he knew "small Latin and less Greek."

Words

J M C

have a few questions that I wish to put before you in your role as professional translator.

The first of these is of an ethical nature. To explain what lies behind the question, let me supply some background information. For a publisher in the Netherlands I am at present editing a novel that was first published, in South Africa, in English, about a hundred years ago. The novel is very long—too long for modern tastes. My primary duty as editor is to condense it before it is handed over to a translator.

Though the author, Olive Schreiner, held political views that by the standards of her day were progressive, she sometimes indulged in anti-Semitic language in a way that is unacceptable nowadays. She also used terms for Africans that African readers today find offensive.

The question that faces me as editor is whether I should

let such language stand, and instruct the Dutch translator to use equivalent racist terminology from Dutch of the same historical period; or whether I should replace the offensive terms with neutral synonyms.

If I follow the latter course, I in effect falsify the novel by giving the impression that Schreiner was free of the racial prejudices that were common among her contemporaries, and therefore that, in respect of race, she was ahead of her times.

The decision is, of course, not mine alone. The translator may have views of her own; and the final decision will rest with the publisher.

In general form, the question on which I would like you to comment is the following: What should a translator—for example yourself—do when she is given the task of translating a text about which she has moral reservations?

My guess is that you will reply that you would not accept such a commission. But let us say that the problematic language is not fundamental to the book. Let us say that it is easily replaced with neutral-sounding equivalents. What then?

For example, if you were asked to translate Mark Twain's *Huckleberry Finn*, would you change the racist terms used to refer to African-American people? And would you do so even if you recognized that Twain was using such language in an ironic way—that the racist language was not his own, as author, but belonged to the slave-holding South that he was critically depicting?

M D

Translation is a complex activity that can fulfill many roles. These roles are generally determined by the aims we are pursuing and the text we are dealing with. As you say, translation is not a one-actor play; often, the translator does not have the last word. From a sociological point of view, we find a commissioner, an editor, and a translator; they are all dealing with a text in its original form. Unlike sociology, linguistics, when asked about this activity, distinguishes between different types of texts to be translated: Is it a novel, an ancient treatise on mathematics, a paper about the future of politics? Reception theory, for its part, mainly focuses on the public, defining translation in terms of the expectations of eventual readers or consumers. All these perspectives are decisive when we try to figure out how a text should be translated and which kind of role translation plays in our world.

Besides these actors and processes, which are objective and well known by the literature on translation, there is also myself as a translator, with my silent possibilities and the awareness I can develop towards my task. Personally, I'm quite a proponent of exactness. The principle of fidelity to the form and content of something that precedes my writing (my translating as writing) lies higher than my own positions and views as well as those of my contemporaries in the target language. Consider the opposite case and make a rule out of it; probably, you will not be pleased with the results.

If translators had not been mostly accurate over thousands of years, today we wouldn't have something like a tradition. Of course, there is the sceptical view stating that in every translation something or much of a text gets lost. According to this view, all tradition consists of a series of misunderstandings based on deep-seated (and wrong) beliefs in something that is called original. Well, this might be right. My point here is to stress that without the attitude of accurateness we would have no passing on across languages. This picture would present to us a world in which a shared past is possible only within each language. I think this picture is not very tempting.

Coming to your example, I understand that the final decision is to be made by the person or the publishing house that has commissioned the edition of Olive Schreiner. As far as I know, publishers also bear legal responsibility. Of course, you are talking about ethical matters and you are principally interested in the personal sphere and not in formal rights. For myself, I would reproduce every view and position the manuscript gives me, even if I utterly disagree. The ethical question marks again the vital distinction—for me vital— between an author and a translator. If I open the door to my opinions on the content, the result of the translation process will ultimately be a commentary, a paraphrase, an editing— but not a translation. The ethics of translation are the ethics of closeness. As you have pointed out, difficulties arise when an original deploys dubious moral contents. These are not the only cases in which an ethics of accuracy should prevail.

Let me explore one last idea related to these border situations in translation. We may consider revolting expressions as a particular case of *zero equivalence*. Equivalence is the product of translation in general: I have a word, such as *house*, and I make an equivalence with *casa* in Spanish. Zero equivalence is when there is no direct or "natural" counterpart for a word of the original, for instance, when the object is unknown in the target culture. It is therefore justifiable that we don't have any equivalent in the target language. Take, for example, the expression *pastel de nata* in Portuguese. Probably, we will just take over the formula and write: "she had a *pastel de nata* in her favourite café." My suggestion here is that unwelcome or morally dubious expressions in the original produce of their own force, in us, a case of *zero equivalence*. This means we have to deal with them as special items in translation, that is, footnoting them with an asterisk, stressing the fact that in our language these expressions should have a special place or none. In the extreme case, which would not be the first choice, you can wordlessly erase the offending phrase.

J M C

I have a more general question about the vocation of translator: Should the translator think of herself as an invisible helping hand, discreetly converting a text from one language into another, or should she be free to play a more interventionist role?

Again, let me say something about the background to my question.

I wonder whether you are familiar with a political movement that flourished in Brazil in the 1920s, that called itself
the Anthropophagy Movement. (I know that Brazil and
Argentina are neighbours, but in my experience there is not
a great deal of interchange between them.) Anthropophagy was a movement of political and cultural resistance
which aimed to recover and revitalize indigenous forces
that had been driven underground by European coloniza-
tion. It called itself anthropophagy or cannibalism because
its plan was to devour and ingest the culture of the colo-
nizing power, and then reconstitute it as a component of
indigenous culture.

During the 1960s the brothers Augusto and Haroldo de
Campos—whom you will certainly know of—developed a
model of translation that used this master metaphor of cannibalism, absorbing European influences and then bringing
them forth again enriched with indigenous elements. In this
respect they are pioneers of post-colonial translation theory.

The ideas of anthropophagy were theorized by the Bra-
zilian translator Rosemary Arrojo in the 1980s. She wrote
that in her translation workshop the source text—the object
of translation (or of reading or of interpretation)—becomes
a kind of palimpsest on which the traces of a past cultural
moment can be erased to make place for a rewrite—an
updating—of that moment. By this means the fetishization of an "original" that must be faithfully preserved
is overthrown.[1]

What Arrojo says here is in line with what Jacques Derrida was saying at much the same time. To Derrida, it is

wrongheaded to think of the source text as a record of an original meaning—a meaning that can be fully and faithfully reproduced in another language. Any dream of perfect translation, translation "without remnants," is just a dream: when the job of translation is completed there is always something left over.[2]

The reconceptualization of translation that we find in Derrida and elsewhere, with a markedly active or creative role for the translator, was taken up decades ago by feminist scholars who retranslated foundational religious texts, first Christian, then more recently Islamic, to make them more hospitable to women. Feminist critics have reconceived the task of the translator in even more radical ways. Are men competent, by nature and upbringing, to translate women's texts, they have asked, or women men's? Furthermore, for the sake of more equitable gender relations, should translators not take it upon themselves to change and improve the texts they work with? Luise von Flotow, for example, a leading Canadian translator and theorist of translation, mentions cases where she felt compelled to change the text to conform to her own feminist beliefs.[3] And the North American translator Suzanne Jill Levine writes: "All [women] . . . who echo"—by which she means faithfully echo—"the ideas and discourse of great men are, in a sense, betrayers"—a new twist to the motto *traddutore, traditore*.[4]

I come to the point. What are your views on the idea of translator as co-creator? I know that you translate German philosophical texts. When you translate Heidegger, for example, and you encounter a line of thought with which

you disagree profoundly, do you translate it faithfully (if I
may again use that old-fashioned word) or do you translate
it critically, by which I mean in such a way that the reader
will have a sense of the darker implications of the text?

M D

I like the idea of critical translation as the technique of sub-
tly stressing the obscure implications of a given content.
The method does not necessarily collide with the principle of fidelity. Indeed, we can convey unpleasant contents
while leaving little instructions for the reader. This can be
done consciously and with elegance, which is, in my view,
a good solution. Most of the time, however, these marks are
left unwittingly by translators; we leave traces of our ideas
and representations when we give a text a new shape in
another language. We make mistakes, we choose one word
instead of another that might be stronger, more offensive,
or the contrary. I doubt that we should leave these traces
systematically and on purpose, making our presence visible
in every step we take. Whether abstaining from taking an
interventionist role, as you put it, is a proof of humility or
not, I cannot say. Personally, I tend to think of translation
as a charitable activity, an active way of giving something
to others and of being extremely productive within a culture. One thing seems clear: as a translator you are far less
emotionally indulgent towards yourself than when you act
as an author.

Movements such as cultural anthropophagy in Brazil are a by-product of remarkable moments in a culture. Ancient Greek had a word for it: *kairos*, the special opportunity. Sometimes in the history of a country or a language, exchange with others accelerates. At such times, the culture becomes aware of a transformation within itself made possible through translation, that is, through the translation of literary, historical, and scientific material from another culture or cultures into one's own. Germany, for instance, had such a moment in the late eighteenth century. These moments of conscious appropriation of foreign contents are rare but extremely profitable; they occasionally produce a theory of translation by itself. It also happened in Israel with the massive movement of translation into Modern Hebrew that began in the 1960s. Principally, the idea of cannibalism applies to each of these appropriation movements. How much we throw away from the original and how much we mix with our own culture is a matter of necessity and a matter of taste. However, there are some constraints. It seems that the distance between two cultures inevitably influences the way translations are made and determines the degree of mixing as opposed to literal translation. The more distant two cultures are, the more likely it is that mixing becomes the only way to make the new content understandable. But this cannibalism can also, as in the case of Brazil, be part of a rebellion against the possible domination of the other through translation. In this case, mixing and transforming are particularly political gestures. Every massive openness to new inputs without mixing them with the native culture can clearly arouse the feeling of being dominated by the new. This feeling is sometimes like falling in love: it is exciting but risky.

As for originals and translations and the role of translators as co-creators, I'm afraid I will disappoint you. While Derrida's position can be interpreted as reasonable in some contexts, I reject his scepticism regarding originals. As far as I understand his theory, he was motivated, among other reasons, by the idea of getting rid of the predominance of the author and generally of the dominant position of subjectivity. In his time, more social, linguistic, and political freedom was expected through this approach. I think it can produce exactly the opposite in our present context, when we need more orientation than in those days in which central cultures such as French and German were experienced as extremely rigid. I would say, now our task is rather the opposite.

As I have suggested above, translators usually leave traces of their presence and choices in the translated works. In most cases, these traces are unintentional. To actively intend to leave these marks can hardly be our aim. If we did, we would not be translating but adapting, paraphrasing, or using the original text to make politics—which is perfectly fair and sometimes necessary, but different from translation proper. If you start considering your "creative" interventions as a rule, you will end up actively writing a new text. I have the following suspicion: once you start making this kind of decision (in this sentence, should I change something or rather not?), you are already doing something other than translation: adapting, paraphrasing, rewriting. In this, I might be biased by my expertise in translating philosophy.

J M C

The most influential theorist of translation in present times, in the anglophone world, has been Lawrence Venuti. Venuti advocates what he calls *hermeneutic* translation (what I have called *critical* translation): a translation, says Venuti, should in effect be an interpretation of the source text, more ambitious than a word by word, phrase by phrase, transposition of the text from one language into another, however sensitively this may be done (Venuti calls the latter an *instrumental* mode of translation, the kind of translation that a sophisticated non-human intelligence could in theory carry out). The hermeneutic translator, on the other hand, is awake to the linguistic and cultural matrix or network out of which the text emerges, and does her best to convey this formative background in the text she produces. Rather than trying to make her translation sound "smooth" or "natural" (usually the highest praise coming from those reviewers who favour the instrumental model: the translated text rids itself of all traces of its origin), the hermeneutic translator resorts to techniques of estrangement to make the foreignness of the text visible.[5]

Venuti's attack on instrumental translation is very much in accord with Derrida's critique of the ideal of translation without remnants. But Venuti's critique is two-pronged: it is both theoretical and political. The second prong of his critique is aimed at the literary establishment in the United States and Britain, which, for reasons of its own, rewards "smooth" translations that create the impression that the book may as well have been written in English.

Let us take a look at the literary establishment that Venuti attacks, and at the publishing industry behind it. We all know that there is a gross imbalance between the anglosphere and the rest of the world when it comes to the publication of translations. I can't quote figures, but in Europe and Latin America and East Asia the number of books translated out of English is huge, whereas in the USA and Britain the number of books translated out of foreign languages is comparatively small. Furthermore, in translations out of foreign languages into English, we find a surprising sameness of style. Venuti attributes this sameness to a consensus that reigns in the publishing industry. Broadly speaking, books that seem too "foreign" in style and content are ignored, while books that are better suited to anglophone tastes are translated into a style of English prose that American and British readers will feel comfortable with. In Venuti's terms, this kind of translation is instrumental through and through, taming whatever wildness there is in the original.

I won't say more except to mention that Venuti's attack on the homogenizing of translation in anglophone publishing coheres with my own unease about the power that publishing in the North, and the culture industry of the North in general, exercises over cultural distribution in the South. My specific unease—which I gave voice to in our earlier conversations—is over the power that the literary gatekeepers of the North (agents, editors, reviewers, teachers, scholars) exert over the literatures of the South.

M D

Venuti has been right in many of his claims. He was one of the first who rebelled against smoothing translations, that is, against producing texts that are supposed to be read as originals. For the publishing industry, this appears to be a desirable feature in a translation. They are afraid of the fact that sometimes translations can inspire the feeling of something strange or difficult. It seems better for the reader to forget that there was someone who made possible the transition from a language to another. This desire for easiness and fluency is rather common. However, it has been said that the degree of dominance of a language is in direct proportion to the degree of smoothness in translation. Recent evidence in the English-speaking world reinforces the thesis. But consider French: something similar happened about three hundred years ago in France. Back then, people were so confident about their linguistic means—the French language—that the best thing a foreign original could undergo was to become as French as possible. Contents were erased, customs were adapted to the taste of the reading public, transforming the unpleasant into pleasing and the tedious into amusing. At the end, the result is the opposite of an enrichment of language: your translation is more of a mirror of your own culture than any appropriation of something new and foreign.

The picture presented by Venuti is still valid today.

Nobody would call into question the predominance of the English publishing industry in our times. The imbalance between linguistic exports and imports gives a strong indication of this fact. Take, for instance, a not exactly minor producer such as Germany: the volume of books translated into German is approximately five times greater than that of books translated into English in the United States, according to figures of the past years. Of those books translated into German, the great majority were originally written in English—for 2022, 60.4 percent were translated from English, followed by 12.2 percent from Japanese and 10.6 percent from French. The remaining 16.8 percent of the total number of translations were made from the many other languages in the world—which, just to refresh the figure, are about six thousand. Moreover, the trade balance with the English publishing industry is appalling. Of the total amount of books written in German language in Germany, only 4 percent were sold for English-translation rights. These figures are more striking when we take a look at smaller publishing industries, that is, linguistic and cultural contexts where translations are more dominant and less diverse. The balance is the opposite when we see the figures for English-speaking countries. It is said that translation explains only 3 percent of new releases each year in the USA, for example. As evidence shows, the need of anything written in another language is low. Universities, for example, are allowed to ask their candidates to provide proof of expertise by evidencing publications exclusively written in that language. Any other intellectual work becomes almost invisible. No wonder that a majority of scientists in the world now write in English. Since dominant languages are always dominant exporters of knowledge and beauty, they are somehow right in their feeling of self-provision; if you produce enough truth and enough beauty in your own language and culture so that you become the primary exporter of these goods, why would you care about commissioning translations?

That reminds us of something usual but still disturbing. Being in a central position, it seems difficult for a culture to step aside and regard itself just as it is. A dominant culture would always try to forget how entwined it is with domination. This we can take as the opposite of the time of openness mentioned before, when foreign languages and new stories are actively welcomed in a given language. Why English has acquired its current predominance has been the object of speculation; I think what is particular to English is the dimension of its reach, which is mainly due to the economic and political structure of our world today. But we should not forget that the global dominance of English does not exclude the regional dominance of other languages over third parties. Take, for example, Spanish. During the first decade of the present century, policy makers in Spain dreamt about the future of Spanish in the United States. According to some predictions, a quarter of the US population would speak Spanish, mainly because of the growth of the so-called Latino community. Spain's interests were mostly if not exclusively commercial: that growth promised a huge market for books printed in Spain. However, things are not going in that direction. The pressure put by Eng-

lish on other speaking communities in the United States is
so strong that people are increasingly avoiding using their
knowledge of Spanish publicly. But, as we have seen, an
oppressed language in one part of the world can be oppress-
ing over others in another part. Spanish used to oppress
indigenous languages and still does today. We should not
forget this fact.

J M C

Thus far you and I have talked about translatability and
untranslatability at a practical level. What we have had in
mind are problem cases: books marked by offensive language of one kind or another, or books that are so dense
with slang and local references that they are opaque to
the foreign reader. I want to push on now to think about
untranslatability at a more abstract level.

As long as we are translating between European languages, instances of untranslatability do not often come up
as obstacles in the translator's path. This reflects the culture
and history that Europe and Europe's ex-colonies largely
share. But as we move further away from Europe or the
so-called West, the question of translatability comes more
and more into prominence.

At a certain rudimentary level, of course, translation is
always possible, even if the two strangers have to resort to
hand-gestures. The claim that translation of a kind is always
possible is the cornerstone of what philosophers of language
call universalism. There is a semanticist in Australia named

Anna Wierzbicka who has backed up the universalist argument in a practical way by constructing a primal or universal language into which any utterance in any language can be unambiguously translated. Thus, to translate between language A and language B, all you need to do is to reduce the utterance in language A to its primal form, that is to say, into Wierbicka's primal language, and then translate it out of that primal language into language B.[6]

I won't burden you with an example of what utterances look like when reduced to Wierbicka's primal form, since the notational system is complex and difficult to master without study. What is important is that she has produced an inter-language of semantic primitives and has tested it on a variety of languages, including indigenous Australian languages. She claims that it works, and furthermore that her claim is empirically testable.

WIERZBICKA'S UNIVERSAL INTER-LANGUAGE IS only one of many realizations, over history, of the dream of a return to a time before Babel, before humankind descended into mutual incomprehension, a descent which has in turn brought into existence the profession of translation.

The opposing argument, that translation is fundamentally impossible, is usually presented through counterexamples. One of the commonest counter-examples to translatability come from the colour spectrum.

The colour spectrum—that band of the spectrum accessible to human powers of vision—is continuous. In theory there are an infinite number of colours corresponding to the infinite number of points on the band. But in practice, human languages break up the spectrum into a small set of discrete bandwidths. Many languages, perhaps most languages, identify blue, green, yellow, and red among the bandwidths and have single basic words for these four colours. However, there are languages that don't subscribe to this division. The South African language isiXhosa, for example, does not distinguish between green and blue. In isiXhosa, blue is treated as a shade of green.

I am not, of course, claiming that blue—"real" blue—is invisible to speakers of isiXhosa. The language is as capable as English is of specifying exactly what point on the colour spectrum the speaker has in mind. But to describe the colour of the sky the speaker of isiXhosa has to provide a qualification of the word for green-blue, that is to say, to gloss the word; and to gloss a word is not the same as translating it. If I encounter the phrase "amanzi aluhlaza" in isolation, I, enclosed in my Indo-European mental world, am unsure whether the liquid referred to is blue or green.

Examples of this kind seem to me to raise a fundamental question about inter-lingual communication. I write the words "amanzi aluhlaza" and I believe I know what I mean. You read the words "amanzi aluhlaza" and you do not know what I meant; indeed, the only way you can find out is by seeking me out and asking me what I meant—that is, asking me to gloss my words.

I would be grateful for your comments. Am I mistaken in believing that we have here a case of untranslatability?

M D

As you say, there can be colour identification without having a specific word to name the colour that has been identified. Recently, neuropsychology has provided evidence about this contended point. So we can imagine and see something (an object, an attribute) without having a word for it. What is special about colours is that they cannot be properly described. Contrary to other attributes, such as big as opposite to small—attributes that can be described by rewording—there is no such shortcut for colours. Red is red or just a position in the colour scale. Or how could you describe red instead? Probably, this is the reason why philosophers have constantly come back to the problem of colours, using it as an example for a liminal experience in perception. Colours seem self-evident and objective while being profoundly personal at the same time. And to answer your question straightforwardly, I don't think that this is a case of untranslatability. After years of practice and meditation about translation, I think it is rather the opposite: translating is for me finding a solution to these extremely difficult cases of equivalence. The rest is pure mechanics. In the near future, what is usually called translation will be made by machines with little or no difficulty. In fact, machine translation is already taking over many of the tasks previously performed by translators.

But let me try to explain one important point, a point that is relevant for all speakers and not only for the ones that are immediately in touch with this activity. Translation, as you noted, does not take place in a laboratory, isolated from any external factors; it is both a technical issue and a historical fact. Languages that have been constantly in contact show that regular exchanges affect the outcome of translation, such that the higher the linguistic contact between two cultures, the better the results. The evidence for this suggests that we might be sceptical about how far translation can go. We can imagine two cultures that had never been in contact, and we will find that no translation is possible. A philosopher created such a scenario (a thought experiment, it is called) and drew exactly that conclusion: that in the case of such radical exclusion, no translation would result. He pictured a native speaker and an anthropologist who tries to understand a single word pronounced: *gavagai*. Since the native speaker utters the word when he sees a white rabbit rushing by, the first hypothesis of the anthropologist is that *gavagai* means "rabbit." But things are not that simple. Right away he notices that the same expression could mean: "a white animal," "something that rushes by," and a long etcetera. Although the philosopher that imagined this thought experiment insisted that his point was not to cover every translational act with a veil of suspicion, his theory ended up doing exactly this.

The opposite of linguistic relativity is called universalism. Wierzbicka's primal language has many ancestors in philosophy and linguistics. Once Latin had lost its hold on European vernaculars, a series of attempts were made to create a universal language for science and communication. The dream of getting rid of Babel is old and has been expressed in different ways over the past three or four hundred years. Personally, I think that the notion that creating an artificial language will get us over linguistic differences is illusory. As we have been discussing during our written conversation, languages are complex entities that can hardly be imposed and generalized by arbitrary rules coming from above. In order to obtain such a thing as a natural universal language, you would need to go into the houses of billions of peoples, sweeping away the bounds created by mother tongues. Who would like to do that? And how could erasing so great and creative a thing as languages be an advantage? I think universalism can be solved without this artificial move. But explaining how would take us another book.

Let me add a last point. Although I think sceptical views are rather mischievous, there is something important in the thought experiment that pictures a native speaker who utters *gavagai*. It reminds us of the mystery and power of individual words. Yes, you can always have a rewording for a word that is missing in your language when you translate a difficult item, an object or an experience uncommon for your culture. But, still, there is something that goes astray when you offer a paraphrasing instead of a unique word.

What would you say about this? What is this magical power of individual words? It might have something to do with our perception of individual objects. But what happens when we try to imagine something through words?

J M C

To respond to your question about the magic of the unique name, let me turn, one last time, to the question of untranslatability.

I was writing something yesterday, concentrating intensely on getting into words a certain quality that belonged to a fictional character. I was sure that the word for that quality existed—I had it, so to speak, on the tip of my tongue. I went to my *Thesaurus of the English Language* and searched through list after list of synonyms or near-synonyms of the missing word. Finally I had to give up. I wrote down the closest approximation I could find, and moved on.

The experience I am describing is a common one among writers of all kinds, and translators too: the experience of being sure that the word—what you call the magic word—exists, but being unable to find it, either in memory or in dictionaries. Every now and again, in the trail of writing we leave behind us, there is a word with a secret sign hovering over it, a sign of shame or defeat: the word on the page is not the right word but a pretender, the younger brother of the rightful word, or maybe just a distant cousin.

If the word cannot be found, does it really exist? Is the conviction we feel that, somewhere or other, the word exists a false, misleading conviction? Is there truly, at this point, a gap between what we can think and what the language is able to express? Does there exist, so to speak, an arcane supplement to our dictionary in which all the missing words are listed, all the gaps are covered—a supplement that we will never get to see?

Or—to be more down-to-earth—does the word that we cannot find in English (or whatever language we are writing in, living in) exist in some other language? Is that the reason why English adopts *naïve* from French and *kaput* from German—because they fill what we feel to be semantic gaps in English? If this is so, then the more languages we know, the more likely it becomes that the phenomenon of the inexact synonym will disappear. Somewhere, in one of the languages of the world, the exact word sits waiting.

But how realistic is this hope, for the writer, for the translator? First of all, how realistic is it that the writer or translator will know more than one or two languages so thoroughly and so exactly that he/she knows the weight and taste and smell of every word in the lexicon? And second, what chance is there that the reader of the text that the writer or translator produces will be familiar with all these foreign importations?

M D

Let me try to provide some answer via the roundabout of a short story. I've read about this case in the newspaper.

There is a former philosophy student living on the streets of Berlin who is said to be in search for "correct" words. He has his dwellings in the eastern part of the city, more precisely at the Berlin Ostbahnhof. I'm convinced I once saw him sitting by the automatic ticket machine on the platform of the Jannowitzbrücke Station, tightly wrapped up in filthy clothes against an icy current that blew across the platform. Cross-legged, he was bending over a huge volume lying open in front of him. His face was covered by a mane of dark hair hanging towards the book, which could have been no other than a dictionary.

We have a portrait of this former student made by a young artist. This artist once went to Berlin streets with the idea of paying some tribute to the numerous people who have no lodgings other than bridges and train stations in that big city; he ran across the youth with the dictionary and asked him about his purpose reading a thick edition of the *Duden*—the official German-German dictionary—one page after another. The homeless youth answered that he used to study philosophy at the university and was keen to write a theory of society but could not do so before getting the right words. Keeping on with formal studies at the university was pointless before settling this issue. Since then he had been consecrating all his efforts to the task, and he had found no better method than a close examination of every word available in German.

This kind of reading system, the systematic perusal of a dictionary, immediately reminds us of a character in a novel by a famous French philosopher and writer; the character, who is presented with more than a touch of irony, has as a guideline for his intellectual development a daily practice: going to the library and reading a huge encyclopedia, beginning with the A and ending, eventually, with the last of the letters in our alphabet. This picture is, of course, intended to show the dubious figure of a person too scrupulous to achieve any substantial thought or comprehension of the world. He becomes ridiculous and the object of our contempt. This could apply to the young man at the Berlin Ostbahnhof, the more plausible interpretation being that he suffers from some malady of the soul, labeled as a psychosis in our days and maybe as a form of melancholy in past times.

I think, however, that we may see the endeavour of the former philosophy student as a legitimate ambition. The story brought me back to an old habit of mine consisting of sticking little yellow Post-its with quotations all over a little apartment I used to inhabit during my early youth. Rarely were these phrases an output of my own writing, most of them being quotations I really liked. Among these phrases I once noted: *Please, bring new categories!* Over the years, this little demand has remained stuck to the blackboard in the back of my mind, while almost all other Post-its are now missing. Here "categories" meant the truly significant words, the concepts that make us think accurately, providing suitable tools to examine people, experiences, and readings.

But who was supposed to bring me these new categories so badly needed, I didn't know. In the resolution of the young man sitting on the platform and exposed to Berlin's icy winter I see this same urgency, and an answer to my question. Nobody but ourselves is in a position to bring the words desperately needed to think according to our present times. Over the years, I have come to this conclusion, which is neither easy nor painless. The phrase now reads: *Go and search for words*. Maybe not following too rigid a pattern like the former philosopher, but with that same conviction. Less desperately, in the more sober vein of thinking about language, its vagaries, pitfalls, and bliss.

J M C

Your young student reminds me of Gustave Flaubert's comic novel *Bouvard et Pécuchet*, the story of two middle-aged men who decide that, as a hobby during their years of retirement, they will become masters of all knowledge. What is it about your student that strikes us as tragic as well as comic? I suppose the fact that we can see him disappearing down a long road that leads nowhere. I am tempted to call out to him, "You do not become a philosopher by knowing words, you become a philosopher by having ideas!" *First* you must have the idea, *then* you can begin to find the words for it.

Yet the young man is not entirely wrong. What is the dictionary of a language, after all, but a map of the universe as the universe appears to the speakers of that language? So perhaps I ought to amend my advice to him: Do not memorize one dictionary alone, a dictionary of the German language; instead memorize dictionaries of two languages, and then reflect on their differences, which are the differences between two conceptual maps of the same universe. Once you have completed that process of reflection, you will not necessarily have prepared yourself for a career in philosophy, but you will be equipped for a life as a translator.

If our two dictionaries provide two different maps of the universe, which one is true, or are both false? We have arrived, unexpectedly, at the Tower of Babel once again. The lesson that Babel is meant to teach us is that all dictionaries, insofar as they are dictionaries of post-Babel languages, are false. The only true dictionary is the lost one, the dictionary of the language that was lost when the impious tower was built: the original language, God's language.

Is that original language, in which each element of the universe bore its true name, lost forever? Not according to the mathematicians. According to the mathematicians, or some of them, mathematics is a language—or a kind of language—in which it is possible to tell the truth about everything in the universe. A proposition expressed in German words is a proposition about the universe relative to the conceptual structure of the German language. It is, so to speak, a German proposition aspiring to be a German truth, neither absolutely true nor absolutely false; whereas a proposition expressed in mathematical terms is an absolute proposition, either absolutely true or absolutely false.

Acknowledgements

OUR THANKS TO SOLEDAD COSTANTINI, PUBLISHER OF
El polaco, who proposed that we develop our ideas on translation in the form of a book; to Miguel Falomir Faus and his
colleagues at El Prado for inviting us to present those ideas
in a lecture at the Museum; and to Jennifer Croft for her
expert eye.

JMC

MD

Notes

I. THE MOTHER TONGUE

1. Stanislas Dehaene, Introduction to *How We Learn* (New York: Viking, 2020).

2. Gilles Deleuze and Félix Guattari, *Kafka: Toward a Minor Literature* (Minneapolis: University of Minnesota Press, 1986).

3. Walter Benjamin, "The Translator's Task," *TTR: Traduction, terminologie, rédaction* 10/2 (1997), translated by Steven Rendall, 151–165.

2. GENDER

1. Marta Lamas, "Feminismo y americanización," in Bolívar Echeverría, ed., *La americanización de la modernidad* (Mexico City: Universidad Nacional Autónoma, 2008), p. 219.

2. "Translating Gender," *NORDA: Nordic Journal of Women's Studies* 6/2 (1998), 134–137.

3. Quoted in Anna Livia, *Pronoun Envy* (New York: Oxford University Press, 2000), p. 6.

4. Steven Samuel, Geoff Cole, and Madeline J. Eacott, "Grammatical Gender and Linguistic Relativity: A Systematic Review," *Psychonomic Bulletin & Review* 26 (2019), 1780.

5. See Sophie Salvo, "The Sex of Language," *Modern Language Notes* 136 (2021), 770–771.

6.   See Elena Dubenko, "Across-Language Masculinity," *Frontiers in Psychology* 24 November 2022, 2–5.

7.   See Anne Curzan, *Gender Shifts in the History of English* (Cambridge: Cambridge University Press, 2003), pp. 46–48.

8.   Roman Jakobson, "On Linguistic Aspects of Translation," in *The Translation Studies Reader*, ed. Lawrence Venuti, pp. 113–118 (London: Routledge, 2000); Claude Lévi-Strauss, "Le sexe des astres," in *To Honor Roman Jakobson* (The Hague: Mouton, 1967).

3. TRANSLATING *The Pole*

1.   For this account see Peter Burke, *Languages and Communities in Early Modern Europe* (Cambridge: Cambridge University Press, 2004).

4. WORDS

1.   See Mary Snell-Hornby, *The Turns of Translation Studies* (The Hague: Benjamins, 2006), pp. 60–62.

2.   Jacques Derrida, "Living On," in Harold Bloom et al., *Deconstruction and Criticism* (New York: Seabury Press, 1979), p. 119.

3.   See Sherry Simon, *Gender in Translation* (London and New York: Routledge, 1996), p. 30.

4.   Suzanne Jill Levine, "Translation as (Sub)Version," *SubStance* 13/1 (1984), 92.

5.   Lawrence Venuti, "Genealogies of Translation Theory," in Venuti, ed., *The Translation Studies Reader* (London and New York: Routledge, 2012), pp. 485, 498.

6.   See Anna Wierzbicka, *Experience, Evidence, and Sense* (Oxford: Oxford University Press, 2010); *English: Meaning and Culture* (Oxford: Oxford University Pres, 2006); Cliff Goddard and Anna Wierzbicka, *Words and Meanings* (Oxford: Oxford University Press, 2014).

Index

acquisition of language, *see* mother tongue

Afrikaans language and the Afrikaner nationalist movement, 20, 22–23, 55

alphabetically encoded languages, 12–14, 41

anaphoric pronouns (gendered pronouns), 36, 39–40, 47

ancient world, xiv, 49
  art and imitation in the, xvii, 18–19, 26
  Greece, xvii–xviii, 9, 72, 81
  see also Rome (ancient)

Anglophone world
  distinct issue of gender in the, 50
  lack of curiosity about other cultures and their languages, xvii, 25
  living as a language minority in an, 22–26
  science as bound by the English language, 67–68, 81, 86–87
  see also English language; gatekeepers of the North; publishing industry; Western culture

anthropology, 43–44, 54, 92

Anthropophagy Movement, 78, 80–81

anti-Semitic language, 70, 73

"anxiety of languages," 37

Arabic language, 12, 15

Argentina
  Argentinian Spanish, xv, 20–22, 53
  lack of interchange with Brazil, 78
  publishing in, 29, 53

Arrojo, Rosemary, 78–79

art, xvii, 18–19, 27–28; *see also* beauty; literature/literary theory

artificial intelligence (AI), xviii–xix

artificial languages, 26, 93

assimilation, through language, 25–26

Australia, 29, 88–89
authority/authorship
    classical imitation, xvii, 18–19, 26
    literary style and language
        mastery, 16–19, 84
    originality and "genius,"
        18–19, 45–46, 71–72, 82

Babel, Tower of, 11, 89, 93, 99
"barbarians," 9–10
beauty, 17–19, 66, 69, 87; *see also*
    art; literature/literary theory
Benjamin, Walter, xiv, 27–28
Berlin, 95–98
bias, xv, xviii, 12, 31–56
bilingual schools in Argentina, 21
Boehnke, Reinhild, 28
Bolivia, 21
Bouvard et Pécuchet (Flaubert), 98
Brazil, the Anthropophagy
    Movement in, 78, 80–81
British empire, 20, 23, 24–25; *see
    also* Great Britain

cannibalism of culture, 78, 80–81
censorship, 63
Cervantes, Miguel, 18
Charles V, emperor of the Holy
    Roman Empire, 65
Chekhov's Gun, 68
childhood acquisition of lan-
    guage, 10–13
Chile, 21
Chinese language, 14–15
Chinese migration to South
    America, 21
Christianity, source texts of, xvii,
    4, 17, 79

"classics, the," 27–28
Coetzee, J. M., xi–xix, 1–3,
    23–24
    on the acquisition of mother
        tongue, 1–3, 10–11
    on the assimilation wrought by
        mastering the English lan-
        guage, 23–26
    avoidance of the term *Global
        South*, 29
    on encountering grammatical
        gender for the first time, 55
    first meeting with Mariana
        Dimópulos, 28–30
    his ancestry of mixed imperial
        languages, 19–20, 23–26
    his resistance to the hegemony
        of the English language, xiii,
        23–26, 60–61, 84
    Jesus novels of, 29
    The Pole, xvi–xvii, 29, 30,
        57–72
    working editing a Dutch trans-
        lation of an Olive Schreiner
        novel, 73–74, 76
    working with translators, 26,
        28–30, 61
colours, words for, xviii, 34–35,
    68, 89–91
communication, xii, 8, 17, 88, 90
    importance of context in com-
        municating meaning, xiv, 31,
        34–36, 40, 46–47, 67, 71
    of medical and technical infor-
        mation, 67–68
    see also culture; knowledge;
        language; literature
consonants vs. vowels, 12–13

content
  act of translation in relation to,
    xii, 69, 75–77, 80–82
  erasure of content that comes
    with dominance, 85
  of an expression, 36
  gender bias, 52, 54
context, xiv
  as constraint to, 46–47
  cultural production and, 67
  historical, 46,71
  linguistic, 36, 40
  understanding gender in,
    31–32, 34–36, 40
copyright, 61
Costantini, Maria Soledad, 29
creolized languages, 67
critical theory, *see* literature/lit-
    erary theory
critical translation, 80, 83
cultural hegemony, *see*
    dominance
culture, xiii–xiv, xviii
  belonging/not belonging to the
    dominant culture, 23, 67
  cultural identity, 9–10
  dawn of human cultures, xiv, 49
  how a culture's self-reflection
    is bounded by language,
    44–45, 87
  inter-language/inter-cultural
    exchanges, xii, 36–37,
    65–67, 81, 92
  kairos (the special opportu-
    nity), 81
  language divorced from, 26, 93
  moments of political and cul-
    tural resistance, 78, 80–81

  the North's control over cul-
    tural production in the
    South, 83–88
  post-colonial world, cultural
    cannibalism in the, 78, 80–81
  shared culture between colo-
    nizer and colonized, 88
  of the world intelligentsia, 3,
    44, 67, 86–87
  see also dominance
curiosity about other cultures and
    their languages, xvii, 25

de Campos, Augusto and Har-
    oldo, 78
Dehaene, Stanislas, 13
Derrida, Jacques, 78–79, 82,
    83–84
dialects, suppression of regional,
    xiii, 8, 66
Diaries of Anne Frank, 69, 70
dictionaries, xviii, 66, 95–99
diglossia, 15
Dimópulos, Mariana, xi–xix
  on the acquisition of mother
    tongue, 4–7
  critique of Derrida, 82
  critique of universalism, 52–53
  dual linguistic life led by, xii–
    xiii, 2–3
  first meeting with J. M. Coet-
    zee, 28–30
  her ancestry of mixed imperial
    languages, 21–22
  on how identity is shaped by
    the Other, 6–10
  on how literary style has
    changed, 18–19

Dimópulos, Mariana (*continued*)
  on markers of social distance in
    language, 36, 58–59
  problem of *El polaco*, xvi–xv,
    30, 61, 57–72
  translating works by Robert
    Musil, 28–29
  on writing as treating one's
    mother tongue as foreign,
    10, 36
discrimination, through language, 7
distance, xiii, 81; *see also* markers of social distance *under*
  grammar
dominance
  belonging/not belonging to the
    dominant culture, 23, 67
  forces of linguistic pressure,
    xiii, xvi, 21, 85, 87–88
  globalization and linguistic,
    43–44, 64–65, 67
  male dominance/female sub-
    jugation through grammar,
    xiv–xvii, 40–43, 47–50,
    51–56
  multilingualism vs. monolin-
    gualism, xii–xiii, 2–3, 8–9, 21
  see also empire; politics and
    power
dominant languages, xiii, 87,
  63–65
  Afrikaans, 20, 22–23, 55
  Chinese, 14–15
  European languages, 64–66,
    82, 85–86
  as the language of science,
    67–68, 81, 86–87

Latin, 64, 92
official/national/central languages, xiii, 2, 7–8, 15–16,
  21, 66
  see also Anglophone world;
    English language; Spanish
    language
Dostoyevsky, Fyodor, 18
Duden dictionary of the German
  language, 95–98
Dutch language, 64, 66; *see also*
  Afrikaans language and
  the Afrikaner nationalist
  movement

East Asia, translations published
  in, 84
education, 7–8
  academic gatekeeping, 44
  bilingual schools in Argentina,
    21
  childhood acquisition of lan-
    guage, 10–13
  "English Language and Litera-
    ture" courses, 23–24
  literacy as tool of the state,
    7–8, 13, 14–16
El polaco (Coetzee and Dimópulos), xvi–xv, 30, 61, 57–72
empire
  colonial migrations, 21–22
  cultural cannibalism in the post-
    colonial world, 78, 80–81
  and the dual linguistic lives
    some of us lead, xii–xiii, 2–3
  fates of indigenous peoples and
    their languages, 21, 54, 78,
    88–89

see also Spanish language;
United States; *specific imperial powers*
English language
J. M. Coetzee's resistance to
the hegemony of the, xiii,
23–26, 60–61, 84
lack of markers of social distance, xiv, 31–32, 36
loss of grammatical gender
from Old to Modern Eng-
lish, 40–41, 50–51
phonemes in the, 15
questioning the assimilation
wrought by mastery of,
23–26
science as bound by the,
67–68, 81, 86–87
Shakespeare's impact on the, 63
in South Africa, 20–22
untranslatability of *gender* in
English, 43–44
words borrowed from other
languages, 95
see also Anglophone world;
gatekeepers of the North;
publishing industry
"English Language and Literature" courses, 23–24
equivalence, linguistic, 35–37,
77, 91
Esperanto language, 26
estrangement, xiv, 81
felt by those speaking minority mother tongue, 3, 9–10,
24–26
as literary technique, xvi,
9–10, 16–19, 24–26, 59, 83

Europe
immigration to South America,
20–22
inter-language exchange in, 37,
65–66
rise of vernacular languages in,
92–93
see also Western culture; *specific
countries and languages*

fatherlands, xiii, 7, 14, 19–20;
see also mother tongue;
nation-states
feminism, xv, xvii, 43–44
female subjugation through
grammar, xiv–xvii, 40–43,
47–50, 51–56
as led by a non-representative
group of young women, xv,
53–54
retranslation of foundational
religious texts, xvii, 79
fetishization of the "original," 78
Flaubert, Gustave, 98
foreign, being/feeling, *see*
estrangement
form, literary, 75
forms of obstruction/vibration
(consonants/vowels), 12–13
France, 18, 61
Frank, Anne, 69, 70
French language, 3, 15, 50, 64–65,
85–86

gatekeepers of the North, 44,
83–88
book reviewers, 29, 62, 83–84
editors, 29, 73, 75, 84

gatekeepers of the North
(*continued*)
world intelligentsia, 3, 44, 67,
86–87
see also dominance; publishing
industry
gavagai thought experiment,
92–93
gender, xiv–xv, xviii, 31–56
gendered pronouns (anaphoric
pronouns), 36, 39–40, 47
gender-neutral forms, xv,
51–54, 74
loss of grammatical gender in
certain languages, 40–41,
50–51
of inanimate vs. animate
objects, 42, 45, 47, 49, 51–55
the neuter gender, 40–42
a non-representative group of
young women leading the
reform of, xv, 53–54
overlapping and intersecting
uses of the term, 40–47
plural forms and, xv, 53
poetess vs. poet, 47–48, 52–53
Sapir-Whorf hypothesis and,
44–45, 48, 92
translating *gender* into *género*,
43–44
"genius," in several senses, 18,
45–46
German language
dominance of the, 82
first translation of Anne
Frank's Diaries, 69, 70
gender of objects in the, 42, 51,
54

Germanization of Eastern
European immigrants, 19–20
J. M. Coetzee's work translated
into the, 28–29
Kafka's poor use of the, 17
Mariana D's translations of
German philosophical texts,
79–80
markers of interpersonal distance in the, 36
phonetic rules of the, 14–16
searching the *Duden* for the
"right" words, 95–98
German Romanticism, xiv, 9–10,
48–49
Germany, 9, 81
globalization, 43–44, 64–65, 67;
see also dominance
Global South, avoiding the term,
29; *see also* South, the
God's language, 99
grammar, xiv–xv, xvi, 38, 66
great writers that wrote poorly,
17–19
markers of social distance, xvi,
31–32, 34, 36, 39
of our mother tongue, 1, 11–13
untranslatability of grammatical subsystems, xv, 37–38
see also gender
Great Britain
empire of, 20, 23, 24–25
publishing industry and literary establishment in, 83–84
market for foreign works in
translation in, 64, 86
see also Anglophone world;
English language

great writers who wrote poorly,
    17–19
Greece (ancient), xvii–xviii, 9,
    72, 81
Greece (modern), 22
Greek language, 72, 81
Grimm, Jacob, 49, 55

hand-gestures, 88
Hebrew language, 4, 12, 81
hegemony, *see* dominance
Heidegger, Martin, 79–80
Herder, Johann Gottfried, 48–49,
    55
"hermeneutic" translation, 83
Hölderlin, Friedrich, xiii,
    9–10
Holy Roman Empire, 65, 66
Huckleberry Finn (Twain), 74

Icelandic language, 25
identity, xii–xiii, 2–6, 8–10,
    53
ideology of Progress, 24
imperial languages, *see* empire;
    English language; Spanish
    language
inanimate objects, the gendering
    of, 42, 51–55
indigenous peoples and their lan-
    guages, 21, 54, 78, 88–89
Indo-European languages, the
    world-view transmitted by,
    49–50, 90
information, medical and techni-
    cal, 67–68
instrumental mode of translation,
    83–84

inter-language/inter-cultural
    exchange, xii, 36–37, 65–67,
    81, 92
"inter-language of semantic
    primitives" (primal lan-
    guage), 88–92; *see also*
    universalism
isiXhosa language of South
    Africa, 90
Israel, 81

Jakobson, Roman, 54
Japan, publishing industry in,
    61–62, 86
Julius Caesar (Shakespeare), 63,
    71–72

Kafka, Franz, 17, 19
kairos (the special opportunity), 81
knowledge, 16
    domination through the pro-
        duction and export of,
        44–45, 87–88
    our perception of the world as
        bounded by language, xiii,
        xv, 45, 46, 91, 93, 98–99
    truth, 28, 45–46, 42, 72, 87, 99
    see also gatekeepers of the
        North; publishing industry
Korean migration to South
    America, 21

Lamas, Marta, 43–44
language, xi–xix, 8–10, 16
    amazing ability to refer to
        itself, 46
    conceiving of null linguistic
        states, 61, 99

language (*continued*)
  as a distinctly human faculty,
    xi–xii, xiv, xviii–xix, 11, 12,
    16
  gender in, xiv–xv, xviii, 31–56
  as the logic that orders and ani-
    mates our worlds, 45, 48–50
  love of language, xi, xiii, 5, 6,
    10, 82
  "native speakers" of a lan-
    guage, xiii, 2–3, 32, 36, 49,
    64, 92–93
  offensive/objectionable lan-
    guage, xv–xvi, 69, 70,
    73–74, 77, 80, 88
  perfection of language through
    perfect translation, 28, 38, 79
  private sphere of language/
    public sphere of social life,
    xii–xiii, 2–6
  temporal nature of, 27, 64
  Tower of Babel and our
    understanding of, 11, 89, 93,
    99
  vernacular speech, 3, 22–23,
    65–66, 92–93
  as a window to a universe
    beyond objects, 55–56
  see also mother tongue;
    words; writing/writers;
    universalism
language acquisition, *see* mother
  tongue
languages in comparison,
  xiii–xiv, 36–37, 54
  alphabetically encoded vs.
    logographic languages,
    12–14, 41

artificial languages, 26, 93
autochthonal developments in
  language, 21–22
consider the dictionaries of two
  languages, 98–99
creolized languages, 67
degrees of inter-language/
  inter-cultural exchange, xii,
  36–37, 65–67, 81, 92
field of linguistics, x, 10–11,
  12–13, 75, 92
finding God's language, 99
Indo-European languages,
  49–50, 90
inter-language/inter-cultural
  exchange, xii, 36–37, 65–67,
  81, 92
language (pecking) order,
  63–65
linguistic equivalence, 35–37,
  77, 91
linguistic relativity hypothesis,
  44–45, 48, 92
markers of social distance, xvi,
  31–32, 34, 36, 39
oppressed languages, 66, 88
prosody of a language, 13
"rootless" languages, 26
Tower of Babel and diversity of
  languages, 11, 89, 93, 99
see also grammar; translation/
  translators; words; *specific
  languages*
Latin, 23, 40–43, 55, 64, 92
Latin America, publishing in, 84
Latino community in the US,
  87–88
Levine, Suzanne Jill, 79

Lévi-Strauss, Claude, 54

Liberalism, 24

linguistic comparison, *see* languages in comparison

linguistic domination, *see* dominance

linguistic equivalence, 35–37, 77, 91

linguistic pressure, xiii, xvi, 21, 87–88

linguistic relativity hypothesis, 44–45, 48, 92

linguistics, x, 10–11, 12–13, 75, 92

linguistic systems, *see* grammar

literacy, 7–8, 13, 14–16

literary translation, *see* translation/translators

literature/literary theory
  afterlives of works of art, 27–28
  Chekhov's Gun, 68
  creative originality, 18–19, 71–72
  estrangement as literary technique, xvi, 9–10, 16–19, 24–26, 59, 83
  German Romanticism, xiv, 9–10, 48–49
  literary form, 75
  literary style and language mastery, 16–19, 84
  literatures of the South, 84
  persistence of "the classics," 27–28
  poetry, 70
  prose fiction, 60, 70

reception theory, 75
  see also authority/authorship; beauty; knowledge; publishing industry

logic embedded in language, 45, 48–50

logographic languages, 14–15

Louis XIV, king of France, 18

machine learning, xviii–xix

machine translation, 91

magical power of individual words, 93, 94–95

male dominance through grammar, xiv–xvii, 40–43, 47–50, 51–56

Marengo, Elena, 29

mathematics, the language of, 99

Middle English, 51

migration, 21–22

misogyny, xv–xvii; *see also* gender

Modern Age, 18; *see also* nation-states

Modern English, 40, 50–51

Modern Hebrew, 81

monolingualism, xiii, 8–9, 21; *see also* dominance; dominant languages

mother tongue, xii–xiii, 1–30, 45, 59, 64, 93
  love of one's own, xi, xiii, 5, 6, 10, 82
  as "natural," 1–3, 5–6, 8, 50
  neurolinguistic evidence about early childhood language learning, 12–13

mother tongue (*continued*)
    and the notion of "native
        speakers," xiii, 2–3, 32, 36,
        49, 64, 92–93
    see also empire; fatherlands;
        nation-states
multilingualism vs. monolingual-
    ism, xii–xiii, 2–3, 8–9, 21
Musil, Robert, 29
mythology, 54–55; *see also* Tower
    of Babel

Napoleonic Wars, 20
nation-states, xii–xiii, 7–8, 13
    Afrikaner nationalist move-
        ment, 22–23
    conceived as our fatherlands,
        xiii, 7, 14, 19–20
    literacy as tool of power, 7–8,
        13, 14–16
    newly independent, 23
    official/national/central lan-
        guages, xiii, 2, 7–8, 15–16,
        21, 66
"native speakers," xiii, 2–3, 32,
    36, 49, 64, 92–93
natural languages, xii–xiii,
    xviii–xix, 28, 46, 60, 64,
    77, 93
"natural," our mother tongue as
    somehow, 1–3, 5–6, 8, 50
"natural universal language," 93;
    see also universalism
Nebrija (savant), 66
neoclassicism, xvii–xviii
neologisms, xiv, 37
Netherlands, 64, 66; *see also*
    Dutch language

neurolinguistics, 12–13
neuropsychology, 91
neuter gender, 40–42
North, the, *see* gatekeepers of the
    North
null linguistic states, 61, 99

objects, 13, 42, 51–55, 93, 95
    art, xvii, 18–19, 27–28
    gendering of inanimate objects,
        42, 51–55
offensive/objectionable language,
    xv–xvi, 69, 70, 73–74, 77,
    80, 88
official languages, *see*
    nation-states
Old English, 40, 51
order of languages, 63–65
original texts, xvi, 26–30, 33, 35,
    37, 78, 82
    creative originality, 18–19,
        71–72
    El polaco as original text,
        xvi–xv, 30, 61, 57–72
    fidelity to the original language
        in translation, xiii–xiv,
        xv–xvii, 28, 58–59, 61–64,
        66, 68–70, 73–99
    see also literature/literary the-
        ory; translation
Other, the, 9–10

palimpsest, the object of transla-
    tion as, 78
Paraguay, 21
paraphrasing, xiv, 76, 82, 93
perfection, pursuit of, 17–19, 28,
    38, 79, 45–46

Peru, 21
philology, German, xiv, 48–49;
    see also languages in
    comparison
phonemes (sounds), 9, 11–13,
    14–15
plural forms, and gender, xv,
    53
poetess vs. poet, 47–48, 52–53
poetry, 70
Poland, 61
Pole, The (Coetzee), xvi–xvii, 29,
    30, 57–72
politics and power
  identity politics, 53
  literacy as tool of power, 7–8,
    13, 14–16
  male dominance/female sub-
    jugation through grammar,
    xiv–xvii, 40–43, 47–50,
    51–56
  mixing and transforming as
    political gestures, 81–82
  scientific truths in relation to
    structures of power, 45–46
  see also dominance; empire;
    nation-states
Portuguese language, 2, 21, 66,
    77
post-colonial world, cultural can-
    nibalism in the, 78, 80–81
primal language, 88–92; *see also*
    universalism
private sphere of language/public
    sphere of social life, xii–xiii,
    2–6
Progress, ideology of, 24
prose fiction, 60, 70

prosody, 13
Protagoras, 48
Proust, Marcel, 17–18
public sphere of social life/pri-
    vate sphere of language,
    xii–xiii, 2–3
publishing industry, xii, xvi, 24,
    61–62, 70, 73–76
  in Argentina, 29, 53
  in France, 61
  global translation trade imbal-
    ance, xvii, 84, 85–88
  in Japan, 61–62, 86
  legal copyright, 61
  problem of *El polaco*, xvi–xv,
    30, 61, 57–72
  role of editors, 29, 73, 75, 84
  "World Literature" category
    of books, 24–25
  see also Anglophone world

race and racism, xv–xvi, 63, 69,
    73–75, 16
reading, the act of, 2, 15, 46, 78,
    85, 95–98
reception theory, 75
religion, xvii, 4, 17, 76, 79
Renaissance, 65–66
Rome (ancient), 3, 63, 71–72
  classical imitation and
    notions of beauty, xvii,
    18–19, 26
  a look at Shakespeare's Julius
    Caesar, 63, 71–72
  see also Latin
"rootless" languages, 26
Russian migration to South
    America, 21

Sapir-Whorf hypothesis, 44–45,
　48, 92
Scandinavian feminism, 44
schooling, *see* education
Schreiner, Olive, 73–74, 76
science
　as bounded by the English lan-
　　guage, 67–68, 81, 86–87
　evidence that gender neutral
　　language defuses bias, 53
　neurolinguistic evidence about
　　early childhood language
　　learning, 12–13
　neuropsychological exploration
　　of colour, 91
　about our individual ways of
　　speaking, 17
　scientific truths in relation to
　　structures of power, 45–46
self-identity, 9–10; *see also*
　identity
semantic qualities of words,
　xiv–xv, 49–50, 61, 88–89,
　95
Semitic writing systems, 12, 15
Shakespeare, William, 63, 66,
　71–72
slang and local references, 88
"smooth" or "natural" transla-
　tions, 83–84, 85
social formulas, 33
sociology, 67, 75
sounds (phonemes), 9, 11–13,
　14–15
South Africa
　Afrikaans language and the
　　Afrikaner nationalist move-
　　ment, 20, 22–23, 55

the colour blue-green in the
　isiXhosa language, 90
mixing of imperial languages
　and living as a language
　minority in, 19–26
South America, 3, 21
South, the, 29, 53, 84; *see also*
　gatekeepers of the North
Spain, xvi, 87–88
Spanish language
　Argentinian Spanish, xv,
　　20–22, 53
　distance markers in the, xiv, xv,
　　31–33, 36
　dominance of, 64–65, 66–67,
　　88
　El polaco as source text,
　　xvi–xv, 30, 61, 57–72
　gender in the, xiv–xv, 39–44,
　　47, 51–55
　linguistic pressure on the Latino
　　community in the US, 87–88
　Peninsular accent, 21
　publishing in the, 87–88
　as target language of transla-
　　tion, 28–29
　translating *The Pole*, xvi–xvii,
　　29, 30, 57–72
specification problem in transla-
　tion, 33–39, 47
style, literary, 16–19, 84
subjectivity, freedom and the
　dominance of, 82

tabula rasa, language as proof
　against, 12
"Task of the Translator" (Benja-
　min), 27–28

Thesaurus of the English Lan-
    guage, 94
Tower of Babel, 11, 89, 93, 99
translatability, 88–89; *see also*
    untranslatability
translation/translators, xi–xix
    adaptation vs., 82
    aesthetic decisions in transla-
        tion, 35, 38
    as co-creation or cultural
        mediation, 79–80, 82–83
    critical or hermeneutic transla-
        tion, 80, 83
    duty of fidelity to the original
        language, xiii–xiv, xv–xvii,
        28, 58–59, 61–64, 66, 68–70,
        73–99
    as enabling *kairos* (the special
        opportunity) for a culture,
        81
    ethics and moral choice in,
        xv, xvi, 58, 63–64, 68–71,
        73–74, 76–77
    false impressions that may arise
        through, 74, 84
    first German translator of
        Anne Frank's Diaries, 69,
        70
    global translation trade imbal-
        ance, xvii, 84, 85–88
    glossing over words, 33, 77, 90
    ideal of "smooth" or "natural"
        translations, 83–84, 85
    instrumental mode of, 83–84
    layers of implicit translation, 59
    literal translation, 69, 70, 81
    of literary style, 16–19, 84
    by machines, 91

(mostly) invisible helping
    hands of translators, 77,
    79–80, 82
nature of a translated text,
    xiii–xiv
neologisms in, xiv, 37
paraphrasing, xiv, 76, 82, 93
perfection of language through
    perfect translation, 28, 38, 79
and the persistence of "the clas-
    sics," 27–28
problem of *El polaco*, xvi–xv,
    61, 57–72
of scientific/practical texts
    vs. literary translation,
    67–68
of slang and local references, 88
as tests of linguistic equiva-
    lence, 35–37, 77, 91
of *The Pole*, xvi–xvii, 29, 30,
    57–72
translators also working as
    writers, 57–58
universalism that translatabil-
    ity suggests, 88–89
wordless erasure in, 77
see also original texts; untrans-
    latability; words
truth, 28, 45–46, 42, 72, 87, 99;
    see also knowledge
Turkish language, 39
Twain, Mark, 74

United Kingdom, *see* Great
    Britain
United States, 23–25, 50
    as centre of knowledge produc-
        tion, 44–45, 83–84

United States (*continued*)
Latino community in the, 87–88
market for foreign works in translation in the, 64, 86
Southern racism, 74
see also Anglophone world; English language
universalism, xv, 4, 12, 47, 52–54
appearance of universalism that comes through domination, 44–45, 52
Wierzbicka's primal language, 88–93
University of Cape Town, 23–24
untranslatability, xiv–xv, xviii, 63–64, 73–99
of colours, xviii, 34–35, 68, 89–91
and the magical power of individual words, 93, 94–95
specification problems in translation, 33–39, 47

Venuti, Lawrence, 83–86
vernacular speech, 3, 22–23, 65–66, 92–93
Vietnamese language, 35–38
vocalization/vocal apparatus during childhood, 11–13
von Flotow, Luise, 79
vowels vs. consonants, 12–13

Western culture, 4
ideology of Progress, 24
neoclassicism in, xvii–xviii

Renaissance, 65–66
shared culture and the question of translatability, 88
Widerberg, Karin, 44
Wierzbicka, Anna, 88–92
women's subjugation through grammar, xiv–xvii, 40–43, 47–50, 51–56; *see also* feminism
words, 5–6
for colours, xviii, 34–35, 68, 89–91
magical power of specific, 93, 94–95
offensive/objectionable language, xv–xvi, 69, 70, 73–74, 77, 80, 88
searching the dictionary for the "right" words, 95–98
semantic qualities of, xiv–xv, 49–50, 61, 88–89, 95
see also colours; mother tongue
world intelligentsia, 3, 44, 67, 86–87
"World Literature" category of books, 24–25
world-views, xiv, 38, 48–49; *see also* ancient world; Anglophone world; language
World War II, 21
writing/writers, 10
great writers who wrote poorly, 17–19
how language influences a writer's descriptions of "reality," 33–34

how language influences our
  authors' personal/profes-
  sional lives, 23–27
as a kind of external memory, 16
poetess vs. poet, 47–48, 52–53
translation vs., 57–58
untranslatability of the magic
  words writers choose, 94–95

writers also working as translators, 57–58
see also authority/authorship;
  literature/literary theory;
  publishing industry

ʒe (pronoun), 53
zero equivalence, 77

ABOUT THE AUTHORS

J. M. COETZEE was born in Cape Town in 1940 and educated in South Africa and the United States. He has published some twenty works of fiction, literary criticism, and translation. Among the prizes he has won are the Booker Prize (twice) and, in 2003, the Nobel Prize for Literature. He lives in Adelaide, South Australia.

MARIANA DIMÓPULOS is the author of four novels and a book on Walter Benjamin. With a dissertation on translation and philosophy, she has translated several authors from English and German into Spanish, among them Theodor Adorno, Martin Heidegger, and J. M. Coetzee. She was born in Buenos Aires, Argentina, and lives in Berlin.